Broomstick Lace
CROCHET

Broomstick Lace
CROCHET

DONNA WOLFE

STACKPOLE
BOOKS

Copyright © 2015 by Donna Wolfe

Published by
STACKPOLE BOOKS
5067 Ritter Road
Mechanicsburg, PA 17055
www.stackpolebooks.com

Printed in the United States of America

10 9 8 7 6 5 4 3 2 1

First edition

Cover design by Wendy A. Reynolds
Photography by Donna Wolfe
Naztazia® is a registered trademark of D. Wolfe Consulting, Inc.

Library of Congress Cataloging-in-Publication Data

Wolfe, Donna, 1974–
  Broomstick lace crochet : a new look at a vintage stitch, with 20 stylish designs / Donna Wolfe.
    pages cm
  ISBN 978-0-8117-1615-4
  1. Lace and lace making. 2. Crocheting—Patterns. I. Title.
  TT800.W65 2015
  746.2—dc23
                                        2015018435

This book is dedicated in loving memory to my grandmothers,
Anna Fera and Catherine Tryba,
both of whom taught me how to crochet.
I'd also like to thank my parents, Robert and Bernadine Fera,
my husband, David, and children, Sarah and Shawn,
for their encouragement and support.
Finally, thank you to my editor, Pam Hoenig,
who guided me with kindness and patience
through the writing of this book.

**Scan to enjoy a video featuring
all the projects in the book!**

Visit http://naztazia.com/videos.html

Contents

Introduction 1

Broomstick Lace Crochet— The Stitch 2

Basic Crochet Stitches 2

Basic Broomstick Lace 12

Broomstick Lace with Half Double Crochet 16

Broomstick Lace with Double Crochet 17

Creating Your Own Lace Patterns with
Broomstick Lace 18

Faux Broomstick Lace 20

Changing Colors in Broomstick Lace 23

Increasing with Broomstick Lace 25

Decreasing with Broomstick Lace 28

Broomstick Lace in the Round 30

Broomstick Lace Crochet— The Patterns 33

Reading My Patterns 33

Finishing 41

Infinity Scarf 44

Pretty in Pink Pillow Cover 47

Boot Cuffs 52

Tote Bag 56

Baby Sweater 59

Baby Hat 63

Cutie Booties 67

Evening Bag 71

Smartphone Case 75

Wrap Skirt or Beach Cover-Up 79

Convertible Hair Band and Cowl 82

So Lacy Wrap 85

Fingerless Gloves 88

Hoodie Scarf 92

Dishcloth, Hot Pad, or Washcloth 96

Ballerina Dress with Tutu 99

Blanket 105

Triangle Kerchief Scarf 108

Slouchy Hat 112

Valance Café Curtain 115

Visual Index 118

Displayed is the broomstick lace blanket that my grandmother made for me when I was born. That's my grandmother in the photograph next to it.

Introduction

Broomstick lace, also known throughout the years by other names such as jiffy lace, peacock stitch, and Peruvian stitch, produces a lovely open lace pattern that works up very quickly. The stitch has been around since at least the 1800s, though its precise origin is unknown. Rumor has it American settlers used an actual broomstick handle to create the stitch, hence the name. My great grandmother made blankets using the broomstick lace stitch in the late 1800s, and my grandmother continued this tradition throughout her life. My love for the stitch began in the late 1970s, after admiring a purple blanket my grandmother had made for me when I was born. I was fascinated by all of its perfect loops and swirls. While I knew how to crochet basic stitches as a child, it wasn't until my preteen years that I attempted the broomstick lace stitch. I made little broomstick lace blankets for my dolls and plush toys.

Over the years, I have made broomstick lace scarves, baby blankets, and various other items for friends and family. After posting a photo of some of these items on my website, I received several e-mail messages requesting that I make a YouTube® video on how to create the basic broomstick lace stitch. At the time I didn't think anyone would have an interest in an old crochet stitch people made years ago, but I was wrong. As of this writing, that video has over 1.3 million views—and counting. You can view my very first basic broomstick lace video at http://youtube.com/naztazia.

To help you learn everything there is to know about broomstick lace, this book begins with the absolute basics of crochet. Although a knitting needle is used with broomstick lace, the stitches themselves are primarily classified under the art of crochet. Next I will teach you the basics of broomstick lace, then how to increase, decrease, and change colors in broomstick lace, as well as several variations on the stitch. After that, we'll discuss important topics such as yarn, gauge, and finishing your items. Finally, you will find a selection of 20 patterns, including wearables, handbags, household items, and baby clothes, on which to hone your broomstick lace skills.

One final note: although the stitch itself is relatively easy to learn and comprehend, producing broomstick lace takes a bit of physical coordination with both of your hands working simultaneously. Recognizing this, the majority of the patterns in the book are designed so that full broomstick lace items work up easily and quickly with minimal practice. In patterns that are more intermediate in nature, the broomstick lace section serves as a nice accent or edging.

In keeping with the modern approach, you can find me on most of the online social media sites. Feel free to check out my broomstick lace videos on YouTube® (youtube.com/naztazia) and visit my website, naztazia.com. You can also find me on Facebook as naztazia, where you can share your photos of projects you make from this book. Happy broomsticking!

Broomstick Lace Crochet—The Stitch

Basic Crochet Stitches

Broomstick lace is created by drawing up loops onto a very large knitting needle (also called a broomstick lace pin by some manufacturers) and then crocheting into groups of those loops. In the patterns included in this book, I use single crochet, half double crochet, or double crochet to do that. Here are tutorials on all those stitches as well as other basic crochet stitches you will need to know in order to work in broomstick lace.

Slipknot

The slipknot begins just about every crochet pattern, including those for broomstick lace.

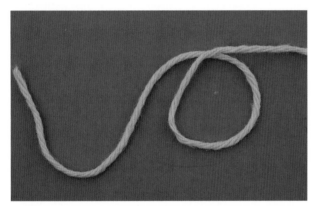

1. To begin, working with the first 6"/15.3 cm to 8"/20.3 cm of yarn from your skein, wrap it in a circle.

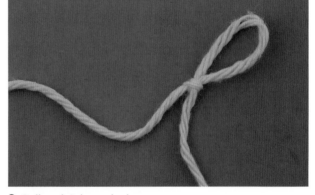

3. Pull and tighten the loop.

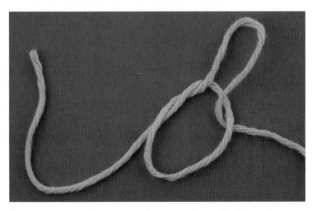

2. Make a loop, then push the loop through the circle.

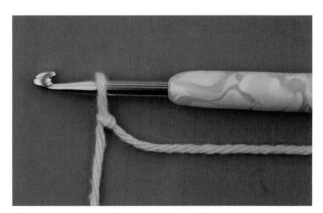

4. Insert your crochet hook in the loop, then pull the main strand coming from the skein to gently tighten the yarn around the crochet hook. You have just completed the slipknot.

Chain (CH)

The chain forms the foundation for the rest of the crochet stitches, most especially in broomstick lace.

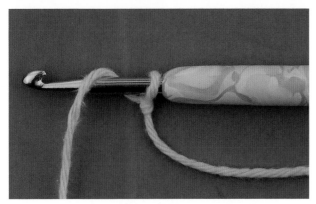

1. To begin, first make a slipknot, then wrap the yarn around the crochet hook. This process of wrapping the yarn around the hook is called a **yarn over (YO)**.

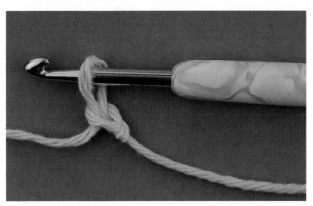

2. Catch the yarn with the hook and gently pull it through the existing loop on the hook. If you have never created a crochet chain before, your chain might be a little too tight or too loose. With practice, you will learn how to create even chains.

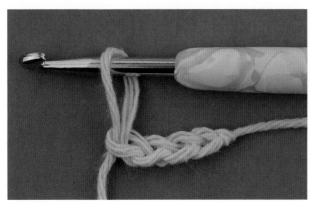

3. Repeat this process of doing a yarn over and pulling the yarn through the existing loop on the hook. Continue in this manner for as many chains as your pattern instructions tell you to make.

When you count the number of chains you have made, the original slipknot should not be included in your count. Begin counting with the first yarn over you pulled through. In this photo, there are 16 chains.

Single Crochet (SC)

After you have made the required number of chains, you are ready to place stitches on top of this foundation. The most common stitch is the single crochet stitch.

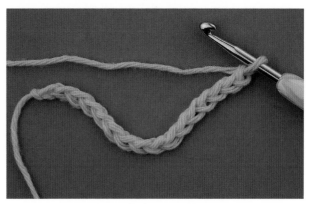

1. Skip the first chain from the hook, which also happens to be the very last chain you just made. Insert your crochet hook through the center of the next chain and out the back of the chain. (Please note that you will skip the first chain only at the beginning of rows containing single crochet stitches, unless otherwise noted in the pattern.) When your hook comes out of the center, be sure you are going under just the back loop of your chain stitch.

(continued)

2. Do a yarn over.

3. Pull the yarn through the back loop of the chain. At this point you have 2 loops on your crochet hook. Ideally, they should be even in height; if not, don't worry, it will come with practice.

4. Do a yarn over.

5. Carefully pull the yarn through both loops remaining on your hook. You have just completed a single crochet stitch.

6. To make the next SC, insert your crochet hook into the back loop of the very next chain.

7. Do a yarn over.

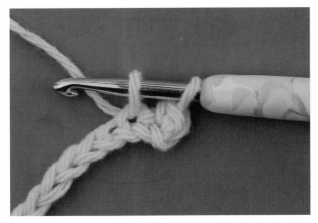

8. Pull the yarn through the back loop of the chain. At this point you have 2 loops on your crochet hook.

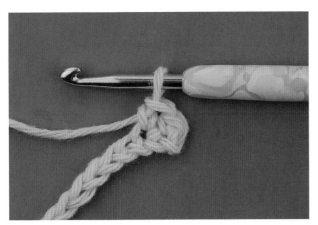

9. Do a yarn over.

10. Carefully pull the yarn through both loops remaining on your hook. You have just completed your second SC.

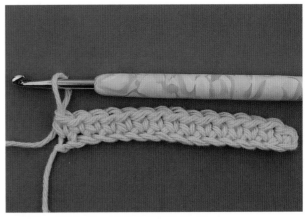

11. Continue across the rest of the chain in this manner.

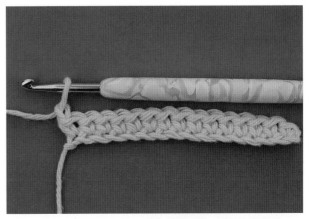

12. When you complete your last SC on this row, you should have a total of 15 SC. To confirm the math, you first chained 16. You skipped the first chain. Therefore, there are 15 remaining chains for stitches.

It is now time to proceed to the next row. To do this, CH 1.

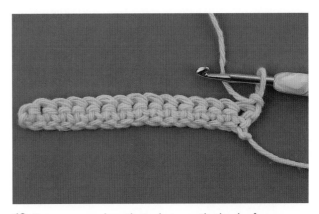

13. Turn your work so that what was the back of your work is now the front of your work. The previous right side is now on your left, while the previous left side is now on your right. The top and bottom of your work have remained unchanged.

(continued)

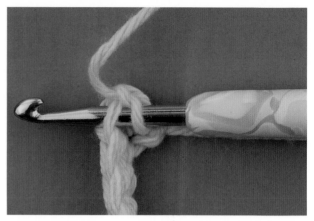

14. Skip the first chain on this row, which is the chain you just made.

Here the crochet hook is being inserted through the front loop of the stitch.

15. Looking at the top of the last SC you made on the previous row, you will see that it forms a loop, with a front and a back. Depending on your pattern directions, you may be instructed to crochet through the back loop only or the front loop only.

For the majority of the patterns in this book, you will be told to crochet through the back loop only, as shown here.

16. Do a yarn over.

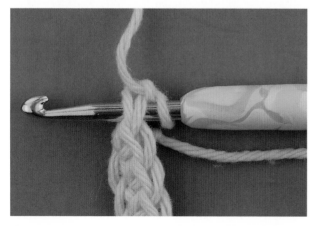

If a pattern doesn't specify, you should insert your hook under both loops.

17. Pull the yarn through the stitch. At this point you have 2 loops on your crochet hook.

18. Do a yarn over.

19. Carefully pull the yarn through both loops remaining on your hook.

20. You have just completed your first SC on the second row. Continue creating SC stitches across this row to the end, then turn the work, CH 1, and continue to SC. The number of SC stitches on each row should stay the same if you are single crocheting into each stitch. So, for this sample, the first row has 15 SC; therefore, this second row should have 15 SC as well.

Half Double Crochet (HDC)

You will use the techniques learned in the slipknot, chain, and single crochet stitches to do a half double crochet stitch; please review the tutorials for them if necessary.

1. Make a slipknot and CH 16 for this swatch.

2. Do a yarn over.

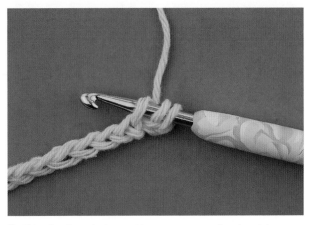

3. Skip the first chain, and insert your crochet hook into the back loop of the second chain from your hook.

(continued)

4. Do a yarn over.

7. You have just completed one half double crochet.

5. Pull the yarn through just the back loop of the chain. At this point you will have 3 loops on your hook.

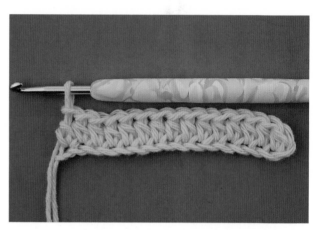

8. Proceed with creating HDC stitches across the row. At the end, you will have completed 15 HDC. To confirm the math, you first chained 16. You skipped the first chain. Therefore, there are 15 remaining chains for stitches. Continue as directed in SC for how to work into the stitches below for the next row.

6. Yarn over and pull through all 3 loops on your hook.

Double Crochet (DC)

You will use the techniques learned in the slipknot, chain, single crochet, and half double crochet stitches to do a double crochet stitch; please review those tutorials if necessary.

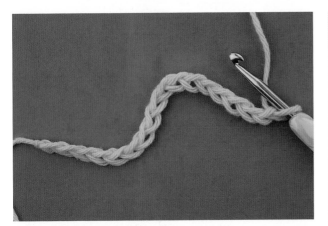

1. Make a slipknot and CH 17.

4. Do a yarn over.

2. Do a yarn over.

5. Pull the yarn through just the back loop of the chain. At this point you will have 3 loops on your hook.

3. Skip the first 3 chains and insert your crochet hook into the back loop of the fourth chain from the hook.

6. Do a yarn over.

(continued)

7. Pull the yarn through the first 2 loops on your hook—you will have 2 loops left on the hook.

9. Pull the yarn through the remaining 2 loops on your hook. You have just completed a double crochet stitch.

8. Do a yarn over.

At the end of the row, you will have completed 14 DC but the 3 chains you skipped will count as a DC, for a total of 15 DC on that row.

Slip Stitch

There are times when you will be working in the round, such as when a piece is worked from the center out (like a granny square) or has a tubular shape, like a cowl or a hat. In such cases, you may be called on to join the end of the round with the beginning of the round. To make this join, you will use a slip stitch.

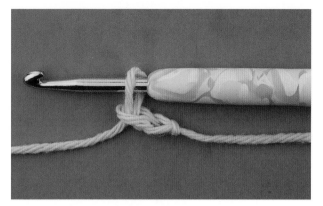

1. Make a slipknot, then CH 2.

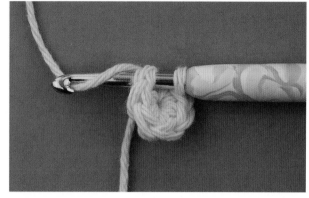

4. Do a yarn over.

2. Skip the first chain from the hook, and make 6 single crochet stitches in the next chain. The stitches will have a bit of a curvature to them. The last single crochet will be somewhat close to the very first single crochet you made.

5. Pull this yarn through, going underneath the two top loops and through the loop on the hook. You have just joined a round of single crochet with a slip stitch. Tug a bit on the loop's base to tighten the slip stitch.

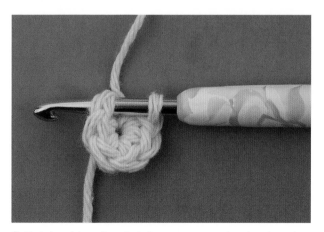

3. To join with a slip stitch, insert your crochet hook under both top loops of the first single crochet stitch.

Basic Broomstick Lace

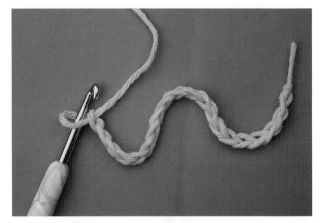

1. Make a slipknot. With your crochet hook, CH 20.

To work broomstick lace crochet, you will need a crochet hook and a very large-diameter knitting needle, U.S. size 17 (11 or 12 mm, depending on the brand), 19 (15 or 16 mm, depending on the brand), 35 (19 mm), or 50 (25 mm). These size needles are also sold as broomstick lace pins by some manufacturers. Each pattern will tell you which size crochet hook and knitting needle you need for that particular project.

Broomstick lace is made by using the crochet hook to draw loops up onto the large needle, then using the hook to crochet into the center of a group of those loops, which creates the broomstick lace cluster, and then repeating this across row or round. The stitch used to crochet into those loops can be single crochet, half double crochet, double crochet, or treble crochet, the most common being single crochet, which is what I will show you in this tutorial.

To keep the stitch count the same from row to row or round to round, the number of stitches worked into the group of loops must equal the number of loops in that group. So, for this tutorial, 5 loops are pulled off the knitting needle, then 5 single crochet stitches are worked in the loops, creating the cluster. For each of the patterns included in this book I will indicate, under Pattern Notes, how many stitches the broomstick lace cluster is based on.

2. Begin Row 1: Slip the loop on your crochet hook to the knitting needle or broomstick lace pin.

3. Insert the crochet hook into the back loop of the next chain. Yarn over and pull through. Place this loop on the knitting needle.

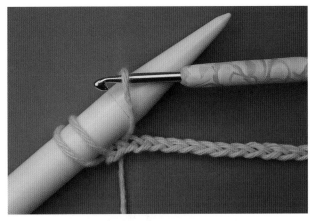

4. Continue this process across the row.

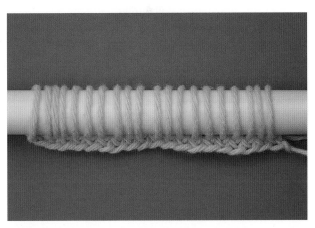

5. At the end of the row, you should have 20 loops on your knitting needle.

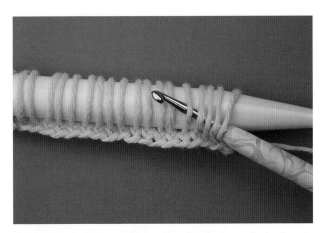

6. Begin Row 2: Insert the crochet hook through the first 5 loops on the knitting needle.

7. Yarn over, pull through, and CH 1. (NOTE: You only CH 1 for the first cluster on a row or round.)

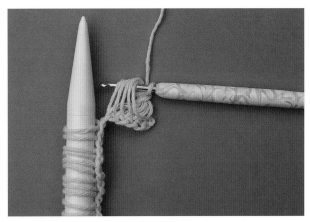

8. Carefully slip the loops off the knitting needle and pinch them together so they do not move.

9. Make 5 single crochet stitches through the middle of the loops.

(continued)

10. Insert the crochet hook through the next 5 loops on the needle and carefully slip off the loops.

11. Make 5 SC through the middle of the loops.

12. Repeat this process for the remaining loops on the knitting needle. You will have made 4 broomstick lace clusters.

13. Begin Row 3: Row 3 is very similar to Row 1, in that you will insert your crochet hook into the back loop of each stitch, yarn over, pull through, and place the loop on the knitting needle. To begin, slip the loop currently on your crochet hook to the knitting needle.

14. At the end of this row, you should have 20 loops on the knitting needle.

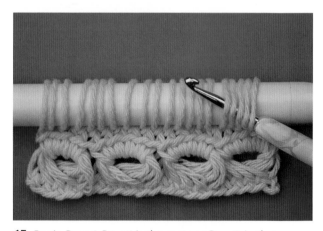

15. Begin Row 4: Row 4 is the same as Row 2, in that you will remove the loops in groups of 5 and make 5 SC through the middle of each group of loops. To begin, insert the crochet hook through the first 5 loops on the knitting needle.

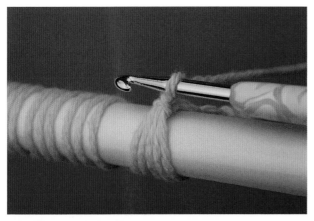

16. Yarn over, pull through, and CH 1. You will only CH 1 for the first cluster of the row.

17. Carefully slip the loops off the knitting needle and pinch them together so they do not move. Make 5 SC in the middle of the loop cluster.

18. Continue across the row as you did in Row 2 for the remaining loops on the knitting needle. Repeat Rows 3 and 4 for as many rows as you wish.

Another Way

Working Broomstick Lace without the Needle

Once you become comfortable with making broomstick lace as I've outlined it, see if this alternative method works for you. After working the first cluster of loops, pull the knitting needle out and continue to work as directed, 5 loops at a time. I find it much more comfortable to work this way and that my stitches are more even. Be careful, though, not to let the loops turn or twist once they're released from the needle. Also, support the loops so they don't pull out. This method works best with yarns with texture; with smoother yarns and threads, you'll have to exercise greater caution to make sure the loops don't pull out.

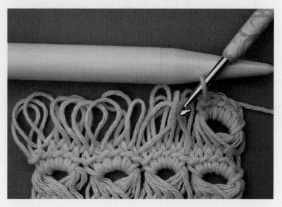

All the loops have been taken off the needle. The first broomstick lace cluster has been completed and the crochet hook is being inserted into the middle of the next group of loops to start the second cluster.

Broomstick Lace with Half Double Crochet

The broomstick lace stitch can be altered in several ways. One way to achieve a taller cluster is with half double crochet (HDC) stitches.

The process is exactly the same as for working broomstick lace with single crochet, except you will be making half double crochet stitches into the groups of loops. See page 7 for a tutorial on half double crochet.

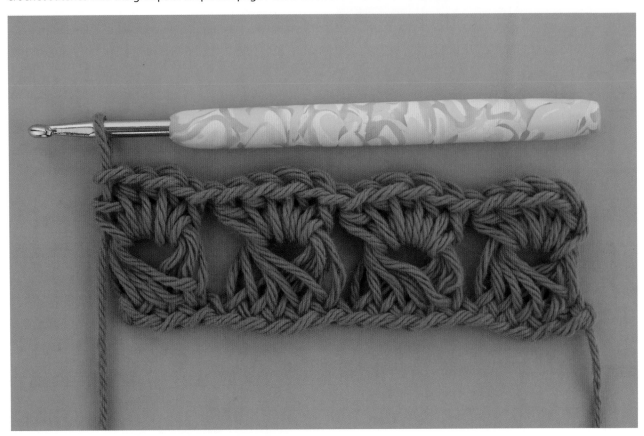

Working the loops with half double crochet makes for a slightly taller cluster.

Patterns that use half double crochet include the So Lacy Wrap on page 85 and the Blanket on page 105.

Broomstick Lace with Double Crochet

For a broomstick lace cluster that is even taller than those made with single crochet and half double crochet, use double crochet (DC). The process is the same as for broomstick made with single crochet with just a couple of small differences.

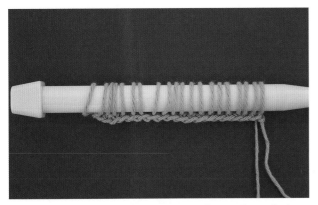

1. CH 20 for this sample, then draw up loops through the back loops of each of the chains, slipping them onto the knitting needle. By the end of the row you will have a total of 20 loops.

2. Insert the crochet hook through the first 5 loops on the knitting needle.

3. Yarn over, pull through, and CH 3, then slip the loops off the knitting needle. This CH 3 counts as 1 DC stitch.

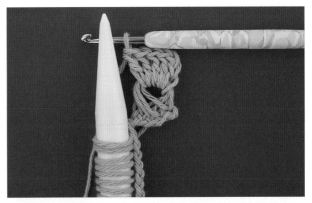

4. Make 4 DC in the middle of the loops for a total of 5 DC for this cluster.

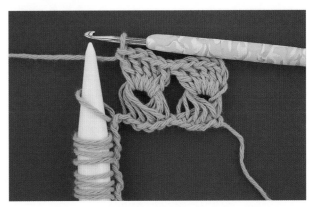

5. Insert the hook through the next set of 5 loops, slip them off the needle, and make 5 DC in the middle of them. Repeat to the end of the row.

6. At the end of the row, turn the piece. Through the back loops only, insert the hook into each stitch, yarn over, pull through, and slip the loop onto the knitting needle. Remember that the CH 3 counts as a stitch, so you will draw up a loop from it also.

Repeat Steps 2–6 as many times as you wish.

Creating Your Own Lace Patterns with Broomstick Lace

Once you understand how to make the stitch clusters that create the distinctive look of broomstick lace, you can have all kinds of fun with the stitch. As already shown, you can work the loops using half double crochet or double crochet for longer stitches.

Here are a few other variations to get you started on thinking outside the book with broomstick lace. These patterns all use single crochet but with fewer stitches in the clusters, resulting in a more open, lacy fabric.

Variation #1

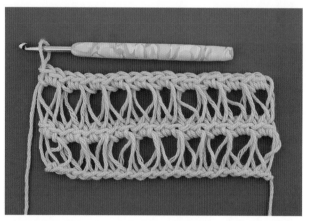

This pattern is made by using a smaller number of loops for each cluster and a U.S. size 50 (25 mm) knitting needle to significantly elongate the stitches. For this pattern, work with an overall stitch count that is a multiple of two.

CH 20 for this swatch.

Row 1: Slip the loop from the crochet hook to the knitting needle, then yarn over through the back loop of each chain, pulling the resultant loop onto the needle. At the end of this row, you should have 20 loops.

Row 2: Insert the hook through the first 2 loops, yarn over, pull through, and CH 1. Slip the loops off the needle. Make 2 SC in the middle of them. Insert the hook through the next 2 loops and slip them from the needle. Make 2 SC in the middle of the loops. Continue in this way across the row. At the end of this row, you will have completed 20 SC.

Row 3: Yarn over through the back loops only of the SC and place the loops on the knitting needle. You will have a total of 20 loops.

Repeat Rows 2 and 3 for as many rows as you wish, ending with Row 2.

Variation #2

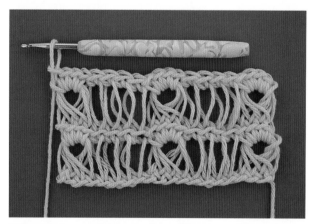

This variation combines traditional broomstick lace clusters with single loops in between. For this pattern, work with an overall stitch count that is a multiple of four.

CH 20 for this swatch.

Row 1: Slip the loop from the crochet hook to the knitting needle, then yarn over through the back loop of each chain, pulling the resultant loop onto the needle. At the end of this row, you should have 20 loops.

Row 2: Insert the hook through the first 4 loops, yarn over, pull through, and CH 1. Slip the loops off the needle. Make 4 SC in the middle of them. *SC into the next loop on the needle and in each of the next 3 loops. Insert your hook through the next 4 loops, slip them from the needle, and make 4 SC in them. Repeat from * to end of row. By the end of this row, you will have made 20 SC along the top edge of the previous row.

Row 3: Yarn over through the back loops only of the SC, placing the resultant loops on the knitting needle. You will have a total of 20 loops.

Repeat Rows 2 and 3 for as many rows as you wish, ending with Row 2.

Variation #3

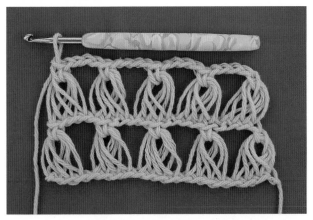

This last variation incorporates chains in between the broomstick lace clusters. For this pattern, work with an overall stitch count that is a multiple of four.

CH 20 for this swatch.

Row 1: Slip the loop from the crochet hook to the knitting needle, then yarn over through the back loop of each chain, pulling the resultant loop onto the needle. At the end of this row, you should have 20 loops.

Row 2: Insert the hook through the first 4 loops on the needle, yarn over, pull through, and chain 5. Slip from the needle. *Slip the next 4 loops from the needle and make 1 SC in the middle of them. CH 4.* Repeat between * and * 2 times. Slip the final 4 loops from the needle and make 1 SC in the middle of them.

Row 3: Slip the loop on the crochet hook to the knitting needle. Yarn over through the back loops only of both the SC and chains and place those loops on the knitting needle. Do not draw up a loop from the very last chain of the row. At the end of the row you will have a total of 20 loops on the needle.

Repeat Rows 2 and 3 for as many rows as you wish, ending with Row 2.

Faux Broomstick Lace

You can create a modified broomstick lace stitch without the use of a knitting needle. This faux broomstick stitch is useful when you want to regulate the size of each loop. In traditional broomstick lace with a knitting needle, all the loops are the same size. With faux broomstick stitch, you can make the first 2 and last 2 loops of a cluster smaller, while extending the middle loop(s) a bit longer. These variations can create a more interesting shape to the cluster.

This is also useful when traditional broomstick lace is too cumbersome because of the need for increases, decreases, and other shaping techniques. While this cluster-by-cluster method isn't difficult, keeping the loops the same size without the use of a knitting needle takes some concentration and is more easily achieved if the loops are kept smaller, no more than 1 inch.

For this swatch, we will make the loops 1"/2.5 cm high.

1. Make a slipknot. CH 15.

2. Pull the loop on your hook so it is about 1"/2.5 cm high.

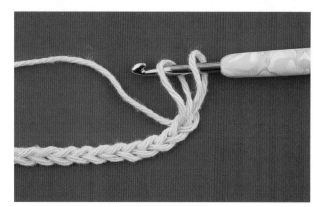

3. Insert the hook into the back loop of the next chain, yarn over, and pull through so the loop is the same height as the first loop.

4. Repeat this process for the next 3 chains, until you have 5 loops on your hook.

5. Yarn over and pull through the 5 loops, trying your best not to change the size of the loops. You may need to pinch them at their bases to avoid pulling or tugging them out of shape.

6. CH 1. You will only do this for the first cluster of a row or round.

7. Make 5 SC through the center of the loops.

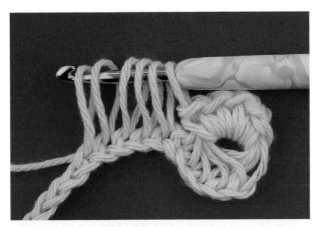

8. Draw up loops in the same way from the next 5 chains—you will have 6 loops on your hook.

9. Yarn over and pull through 5 loops—you will have 2 loops on your hook.

10. Yarn over and pull through the remaining loops. You have just completed 1 SC by using the original loop from the last SC stitch combined with the yarn just pulled through the 5 loops.

11. Make 4 SC in the middle of the loops.

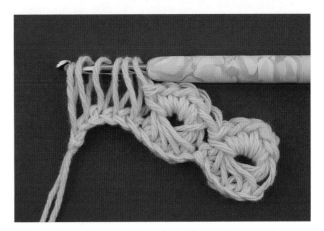

12. Repeat Steps 8–11 to work the last 5 chains and complete the third cluster.

(continued)

13. CH 1 and turn your work.

14. SC in the front loop of each stitch across.

15. Turn the work and pull the loop on your hook so that it is about 1"/2.5 cm high.

16. Using the back loops only, draw up loops in the next 4 stitches, each 1"/2.5 cm high.

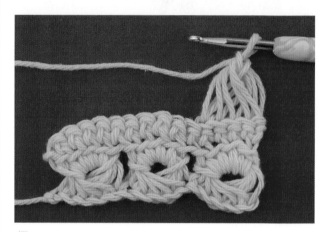

17. Yarn over and pull through all 5 loops on your hook. CH 1.

18. Repeat the process from Step 7 for as many rows as you wish.

Changing Colors in Broomstick Lace

Alternating rows of colors in broomstick lace requires no cutting and weaving in of ends for every row. Simply change to the new color at the end of a single/half double/double crochet row and carry the previous color along the edge if you'll be picking it up and using it again in the next 4 to 5 rows. Any further than that, and you should fasten off the yarn and reconnect it again when needed. And if you won't be using the color again, cut the yarn and weave in the end.

For this sample, we'll work in single crochet with two different yarns, Color A and Color B.

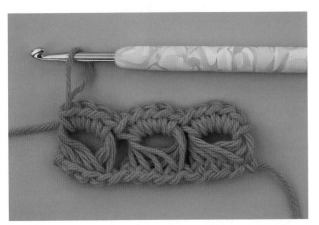

1. With Color A, make a slipknot, then make the required number of chains according to the pattern; in this case, CH 15. Slip the loop on your crochet hook onto the knitting needle. Draw up one loop from each of the remaining 14 chains—you should have 15 loops on your knitting needle. Work the first two 5-loop clusters, making 5 SC in each. For the last set of 5 loops, make 4 SC, then stop.

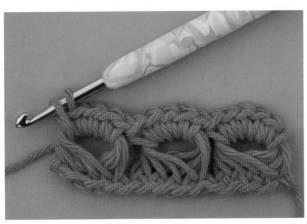

2. Insert the crochet hook through the loops, yarn over, and pull through.

3. Take Color B and form a slight loop.

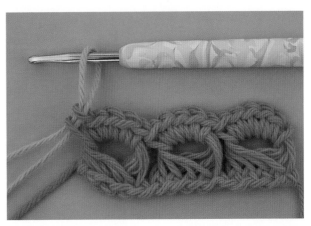

4. With the crochet hook, grab Color B and pull it through the 2 loops remaining on the hook to complete the single crochet. NOTE: If the broomstick lace cluster is comprised of half double crochet, pull Color B through the last 3 loops remaining on the hook. For double or treble crochet, complete the stitch until 2 loops remain on the hook. Grab Color B and pull it through the last 2 loops on the hook.

(continued)

5. Slip the loop from the crochet hook to the knitting needle. You may have to tug on both the old and new color yarns to adjust them so they are neither too loose nor too tight.

8. Drop Color B and pick up Color A. Yarn over with Color A and pull through the remaining two loops on your hook to complete the last SC. Adjust the tension on both Color A and B so there is no pulling in the fabric along the edge.

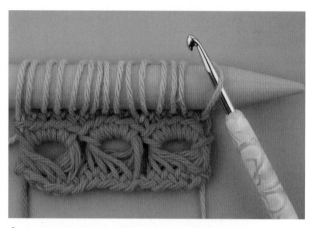

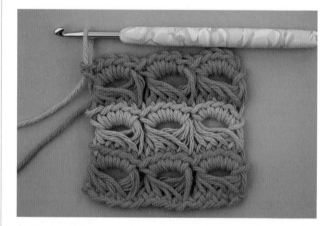

6. Continue drawing up loops and placing them on the knitting needle using Color B to the end of the row.

9. Repeat this alternating color process as you like.

7. Work the first two 5-loop clusters, making 5 SC in each. For the last set of 5 loops, make 4 SC, then insert the hook through the loops, yarn over, and pull through.

Increasing with Broomstick Lace

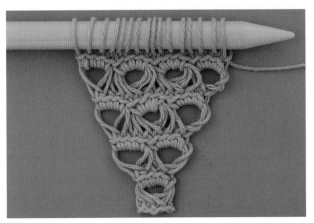

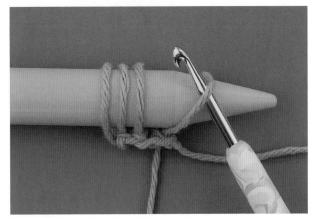

When shaping a piece, you may need to increase while working the broomstick lace pattern. It's really an easy process and you can adapt the directions for the sample below to your particular pattern. To form the triangle shown, we'll first work with an even number of stitches in each cluster. Next, we'll divide the number of loops in each cluster by 2. That number tells us how many loops we'll work at the beginning and end of the row to increase. While we're working with 4 loops in each cluster for the sample, you can use any even number, such as 6 or 8. Also, feel free to substitute the single crochet stitches in each cluster with half double, double, or treble crochet.

This sample is worked in single crochet, with broomstick lace clusters of 4 stitches.

2. Slip the loop on the crochet hook to the knitting needle. In the back loop of each of the remaining 3 chains, yarn over, pull through, and slip the loop onto the knitting needle, for a total of 4 loops on the needle.

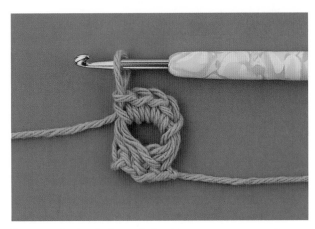

3. Insert the hook through the 4 loops, yarn over, pull through, and CH 1. Make 4 SC through the middle of the loops. You have made a single broomstick lace cluster consisting of 4 SC.

1. For this sample, CH 4.

(continued)

Slipping the final loop of the row onto the knitting needle.

4. Slip the loop on your crochet hook to the knitting needle. Through the back loops only, draw up a loop from each of the next 3 stitches, placing them on the needle, for a total of 4 loops.

7. Slip the remaining 2 loops off the needle and make 4 SC through the middle of them. At the end of this row, you will have two broomstick lace clusters, each with 4 SC, for an increase of one broomstick lace cluster and 4 SC over the previous row. NOTE: When increasing, the increases will be worked at the beginning and the end of the cluster rows, and the stitches in between will be worked as usual.

5. Insert the hook through the first 2 loops on the needle, yarn over, pull through, and CH 1. Slip the loops off the needle.

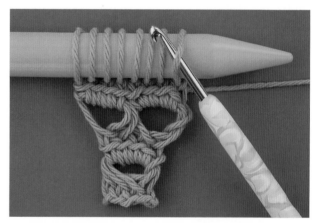

8. Repeat Step 4. At the end of this row, there will be 8 loops on your knitting needle.

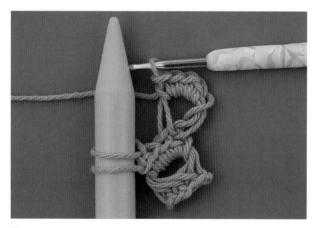

6. Do 4 SC through the middle of the 2 loops.

9. Insert the hook through the first 2 loops on the needle, yarn over, pull through, and CH 1. Slip the loops off the needle and do 4 SC through the loops.

10. Slip the next 4 loops off the knitting needle and do 4 SC through the middle of them.

11. Slip the remaining 2 loops off the needle and make 4 SC through the middle of them. At the end of this row, you will have completed 3 broomstick lace clusters consisting of 12 SC, an increase of one cluster and 4 stitches over the previous row.

12. Continue on in this manner as needed, increasing only in the first 2 and last 2 loops of each row.

Decreasing with Broomstick Lace

Your broomstick lace piece can also be shaped using decreases. As with increasing, decreasing allows you to create shapes that are beyond basic squares and rectangles. We'll address one method for decreasing with broomstick lace below.

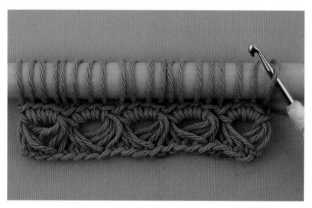

For this sample, we will start with 5 broomstick lace clusters consisting of 4 single crochet stitches each. After Row 3, you will have 20 loops on your knitting needle.

1. Insert the crochet hook through the first 4 loops on the knitting needle, yarn over, pull through, and CH 1. Slip the loops off the needle.

2. Make 2 SC through the middle of the loops.

3. Slip the next 4 loops from the needle and do 4 SC through the middle of them. Repeat for the next two sets of 4 loops.

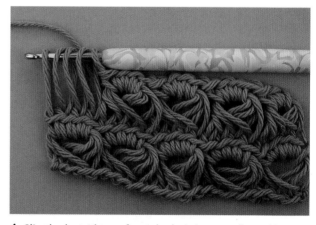

4. Slip the last 4 loops from the knitting needle and insert the crochet hook through them.

5. Yarn over and pull through, then make 2 SC in the middle of them. At the end of this row, you will have 5 broomstick lace clusters consisting of 16 SC, a decrease of 4 stitches from the previous row. NOTE: Decreases will only occur in the first and last clusters of each row. The clusters in between will be worked as usual.

8. Slip the next 4 loops from the needle and make 4 SC through the middle of them. Repeat for the next set of 4 loops.

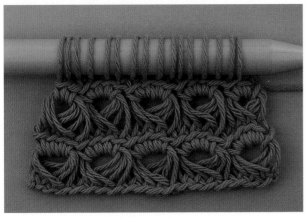

6. Using the back loops only, draw up 1 loop from each stitch, placing the loops onto the knitting needle, for a total of 16 loops.

9. Slip the last 4 loops from the needle and make 2 SC in the middle of them. This completed row contains four broomstick lace clusters consisting of 12 SC, a decrease of one cluster and 4 stitches from the previous row.

7. Insert the crochet hook through the first 4 loops on the knitting needle, yarn over, pull through, and CH 1. Slip the loops off the needle, then make 2 SC through the middle of the loops.

10. You can continue on in this manner as needed, decreasing at the beginning and the end of the cluster rows.

Broomstick Lace in the Round

You'll use this technique for garments like mitts, as well as pieces that are worked from the center out, like a hat, rug, or hot pad. To work in the round, depending on how many stitches are involved, you will need a circular U.S. size 19, 35, or 50 (15, 19, or 25 mm) knitting needle or three or four 10"/25.5 cm or 14"/35.5 cm knitting needles.

This sample will start with a double crochet base, with the broomstick lace worked in single crochet on multiple needles.

Round 1

CH 5. Make 11 DC in the fifth chain from the hook. The chain will count as a DC. Slip stitch to the first DC to join the round. You will have completed a total of 12 DC.

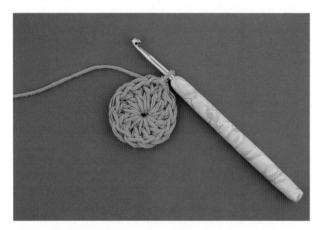

Completed first round.

Round 2

CH 3. Work 1 DC in the same space. In each DC around, work 2 DC. Slip stitch to the first DC to join the round. You will have completed a total of 24 DC.

Completed second round.

Round 3

CH 3. Work 1 DC in the same space. In next DC, work 1 DC. *In next DC work 2 DC. In next DC work 1 DC.* Repeat between * and * around. Slip stitch to first DC to join the round. Transfer the loop from your hook onto one of the knitting needles.

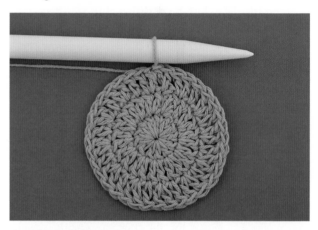

Completed third round.

Round 4

As in the basic broomstick lace stitch, draw up loops and place them on the knitting needle. Because the shape of the piece is round and the needle is straight, you may only be able to fit 9 to 12 loops comfortably on it.

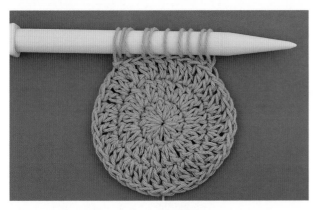

Loops pulled up onto the first knitting needle.

When you have reached the point where the loops are pulling against the needle, begin placing them on the second needle.

Loops pulled up onto the second knitting needle.

Continue pulling the loops up in this manner.

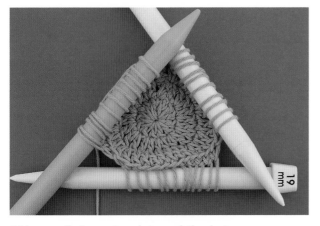

All loops pulled up and ready to work the clusters.

For this sample, begin the broomstick lace by inserting your crochet hook under the first 3 loops near the point of the last-used knitting needle and CH 1.

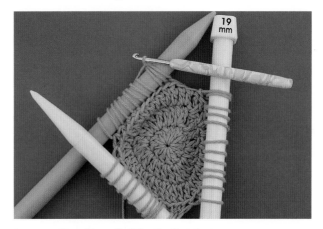

Loops gathered to pull off for the first cluster.

Pull the loops off and make 5 SC in the middle of these loops. The increase of SC stitches is due to the need to keep a flattened circular shape.

First cluster completed.

(continued)

Continue on in this manner and when you have worked all the loops from the first needle, move on to the loops on the next knitting needle.

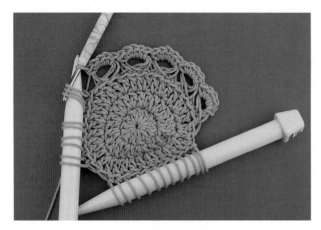

Working the loops from the second needle.

Once all the loops have been worked, make a slip stitch to the top of the first SC to join the round.

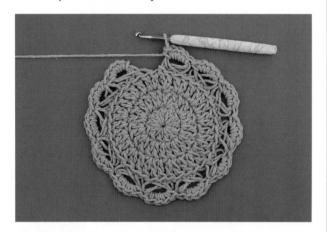

All of the loops have been worked.

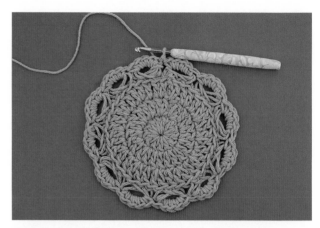

The completed joined round.

You can also work broomstick lace in the round using circular needles, which is considerably less awkward than managing 3 or 4 huge needles.

Broomstick Lace Crochet—The Patterns

Reading My Patterns

Preparation is always a useful step in any project, so please read this section before starting any of the patterns that follow to ensure best results and a happy crocheting experience!

Yarn & Yarn Substitution

Years ago, yarn manufacturers produced yarn and thread sizes according to their own standards. Some gave names to the weights of yarn such as "sport" or "baby," which may or may not have corresponded to the exact size of another manufacturer's standards. To help standardize yarn weights across fiber manufacturers, the Craft Yarn Council of America created guidelines along with easy-to-read symbols for consumers (see the chart at right).

In each of my patterns, I list the particular brand of yarn I used to make the item pictured and I also include the yarn weight as well as the fiber content of the yarn I used. That way, if you decide you'd rather use another yarn for the project, you can choose one of the same weight and a similar or the same fiber content. You will find the fiber content listed on every yarn or crochet thread label. Some labels also include the yarn weight, but in some cases you may have to look it up online on the manufacturer's website.

Understanding Fiber Content

Yarn and thread can be comprised of natural or man-made fibers, or a combination of the two. The fiber content you choose should be based on personal preference, since the broomstick lace stitch itself usually works great with any kind of fiber. Some fibers will feel softer against your skin, while others will have more heft and be sturdier, a possible plus for a project that will get a lot of use.

Yarn Weights

Symbol	Description
0 LACE	Lace weight yarn. Size 10 crochet thread.
1 SUPER FINE	Super fine weight yarn. Sock yarn. Fingering yarn. Size 3 crochet thread.
2 FINE	Fine weight yarn. Sport yarn. Baby yarn.
3 LIGHT	Light weight yarn. DK yarn. Light worsted yarn.
4 MEDIUM	Medium weight yarn. Worsted yarn. Afghan yarn. Aran yarn.
5 BULKY	Bulky weight yarn. Chunky yarn. Craft yarn. Rug yarn.
6 SUPER BULKY	Super bulky weight yarn. Roving.
7 JUMBO	Jumbo weight yarn. Roving.

Symbol source: Craft Yarn Council's www.YarnStandards.com.

From left to right, samples of cotton, bamboo, wool, alpaca, silk, and acrylic yarns.

NATURAL PLANT FIBERS

Cotton: Cotton yarn is one of the most common of the natural plant fibers available in craft stores and yarn specialty shops today. Cotton is a very good choice for clothing items that will be worn or used against sensitive skin, such as baby items. Both cotton yarn and cotton crochet thread are relatively inexpensive and come in a wide variety of colors.

Bamboo: Bamboo is becoming more readily available in both craft and yarn shops. Silky and smooth, bamboo is extremely gentle against sensitive skin. Since bamboo is easily grown and requires very little care, it is a top choice for those who favor sustainable resources and eco-friendly fiber materials.

Other plant fibers: Other plant-based fibers such as jute, ramie, linen, and hemp can be used with broomstick lace. You may have to search them out at your local yarn specialty shop or online.

NATURAL ANIMAL FIBERS

Wool: Sheep's wool is probably the most popular and widely available natural animal fiber today. Items made from wool are known to hold in body heat, making it a great choice for projects meant to keep you warm. For those who like to hand dye yarn, wool is a great choice as it readily accepts dye, whether you're using a commercial dye or a children's flavored drink mix solution to do the coloring.

Alpaca: Alpaca fiber is extremely soft and can be found in some craft stores and most yarn shops. Since it contains no lanolin, those with allergies or other sensitivities might find it an excellent alternative to sheep's wool. Alpaca is very warm and holds up nicely even with heavy use.

Other natural animal fibers: Silk is both strong and beautiful. You can also find yarn made from fibers obtained from angora rabbits, cashmere goats, angora goats (this is mohair), or muskox (called qiviut). Your best resource for these is your local specialty yarn store or online.

Choosing Yarns for Young Ones

Since a baby's skin is soft and sensitive, take care in your choice of fiber. One hundred percent cotton yarn is usually the safest choice for those with very sensitive skin, though many manufacturers now make very soft 100% acrylic yarns that feel comfortable against even the most delicate skin. Acrylic yarn has the added benefit of being machine washable. It is always a good idea to check with a parent or guardian as to what fiber works best for their little one.

MAN-MADE FIBERS

Acrylic: This is the most common type of yarn you will find in craft stores. It is inexpensive, mold-resistant, relatively soft, and holds up nicely in both the washer and a low-temp dryer.

Blends: Oftentimes you will find a blend of materials used to produce yarn. One common blend among the natural plant fibers is cotton with a touch of man-made spandex, which helps give the yarn a bit of stretch. Another common blend is cotton and acrylic, which produces a soft, breathable yet durable yarn, nice for those with sensitive skin. Wool and acrylic are oftentimes paired up as well, resulting in a yarn that can be machine washed without danger of shrinking. Thin metallic thread is sometimes spun in with both natural and man-made fibers to add a little sparkle to the yarn.

Needles & Hooks

Each pattern will tell you the size knitting needle/broomstick lace pin and crochet hook you will need.

Knitting Needles/Broomstick Lace Pins

With broomstick lace, you will be using large-diameter knitting needles, U.S. size 17 (11 or 12 mm, depending on the brand), 19 (15 or 16 mm, depending on the brand), 35 (19 mm), or 50 (25 mm), which are also sold as broomstick lace pins by some manufacturers. These large needles are most commonly available in aluminum, bamboo, and plastic, with plastic being the most readily available choice.

Knitting needles come in several lengths. With broomstick lace, since you will be placing a good number of stitches on a knitting needle, you will want to purchase the longest size available, which is usually 14"/15.5 cm.

Crochet Hooks

Crochet hooks come in a variety of materials, each with their own particular properties (below are some quick guidelines on them). The material you choose is up to you.

- Aluminum hooks are readily available, durable, and are generally inexpensive. They are a bit heavier in the hand, as compared to other materials like plastic or bamboo.
- Also widely available, bamboo hooks are slightly more expensive than their aluminum counterparts and not quite as durable. However, bamboo has a nice, lightweight feel in the hand, plus it is warmer to the touch.
- Plastic hooks are usually the least expensive of all the hook choices. Acrylic hooks are very smooth and allow yarn to glide over them very easily. Sometimes this

(continued on page 38)

Knitting needles for broomstick lace.

Alternatives to a Broomstick Lace Pin

If you can't find your needle or prefer not to invest in one, here are some creative alternatives.

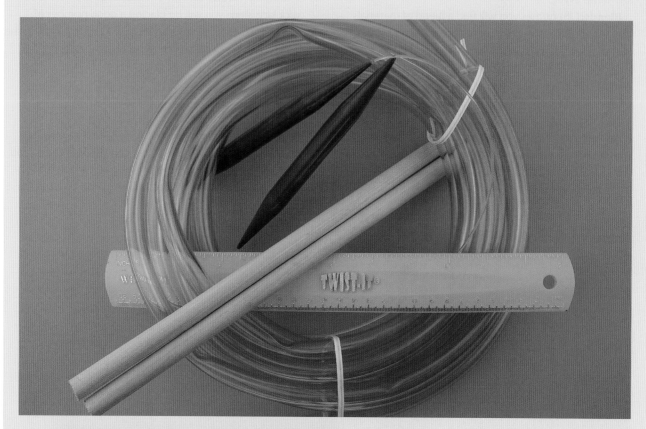

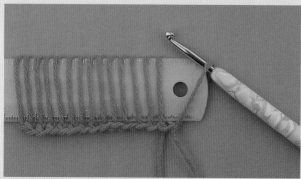

School Ruler

You want a ruler with a smooth surface so that you can easily slide your stitches on and off. If you have a wooden ruler, sand down any rough edges with a nail file or very fine sandpaper.

To use a school ruler, place the loops on the ruler in the same manner as you would using a knitting needle.

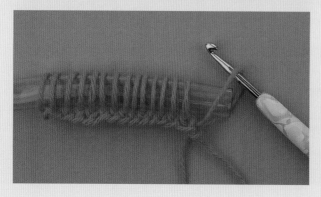

Plastic Tubing

Plastic tubing can be found in most hardware or home improvement stores, usually in the plumbing and pipe section. Most tubing is sized in inches and millimeters and you'll be able to find one that comes close to the measurement of a large knitting needle.

Ideally, the tubing you select should have a smooth surface and be rigid enough to support yarn loops without bending significantly or flattening.

Circular Knitting Needle

A circular knitting needle is preferable when you are working on a very large broomstick lace blanket or bedspread and need to place hundreds of loops on a knitting needle. The cable between the two pointed ends allows the weight of the piece to sit in your lap instead of entirely on the knitting needle, which can cause stress to your wrist.

Don't worry about the loops becoming deformed when they make their way onto the thin cable in between the points on a circular knitting needle. When you proceed to take off the loops in groups, the loops will straighten out when they are pulled back onto the needle.

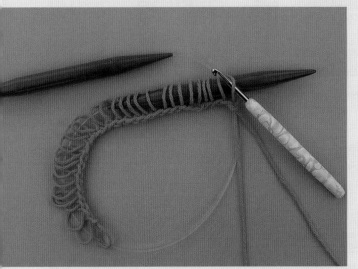

Craft Dowels

It is so easy to make your own wooden broomstick lace pin from a craft dowel. Craft dowels come in a wide variety of diameters—in even more sizes than knitting needles—and you can cut them to exactly the length you want. You can find them in the woodworking section of most craft stores as well as in hardware and home improvement stores.

For use with broomstick lace, you can simply cut the dowels to the length you wish using a ratchet pruner, pipe cutter, small mitre saw, or a mini hacksaw and use it as is. Or, you can taper the dowels to a traditional knitting needle point using a pencil sharpener, utility knife, or file, then glue a wooden bead at the other end to serve as a stopper. Use a nail file or very fine sandpaper to smooth out any rough edges so that your yarn loops do not become snagged.

I have found that applying a conditioner to the wood also helps allow the stitches to slide more easily. One of the simplest products to apply is hand cream. Another option is to rub a sheet of wax paper up and down the dowel. The warmth from your hands will help deposit small amounts of wax evenly over the dowel.

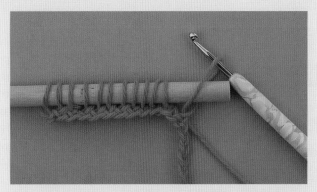

Once your dowel is cut, smoothed, and conditioned, you can use it just like a regular knitting needle in your broomstick lace projects.

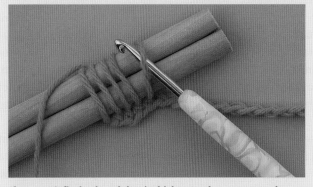

If you can't find a dowel that is thick enough, you can work with 2 dowels at the same time.

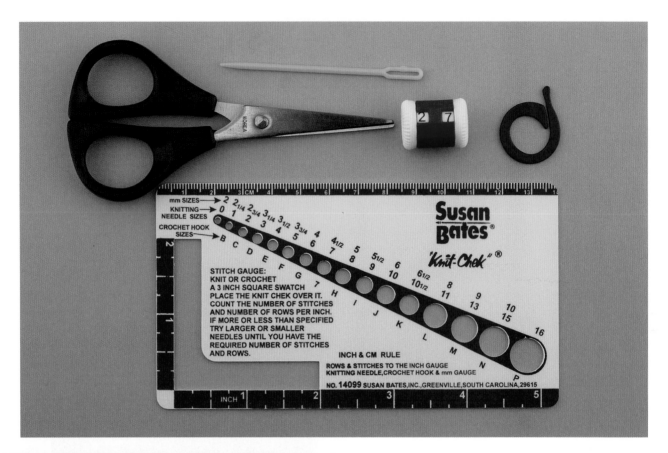

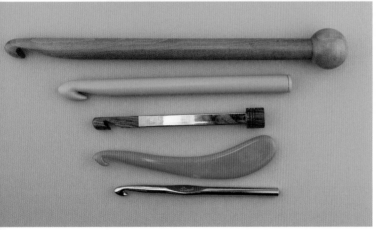

usually positive characteristic can be a negative if your yarn is very slippery. In such cases, an aluminum or bamboo hook might be a better choice, since each provides just enough friction to help hold the yarn steady on the hook.

Like knitting needles, crochet hooks come in a variety of sizes. Each usually has a letter associated with it, e.g. U.S. size F-5 crochet hook, as well as a corresponding metric measurement in millimeters, e.g. 3.75 mm. All of the patterns listed in this book will recommend a particular crochet hook size. However, depending upon how tightly or loosely you crochet, you may need to adjust this recom-

mended size either upwards or downwards to achieve the proper gauge for the pattern (see page 39). If the pattern recommends a size H-8 (5 mm) crochet hook, but you crochet very tightly, you might want to try a size larger, such as an I-9 (5.5 mm) or J-10 (6.0 mm) crochet hook instead. However, if you crochet very loosely, you might need to switch to a smaller size, such as an F-5 (3.75 mm) or a G-6 (4.0 mm) hook.

Other Materials

Yarn needles: Once you have completed your project, you will need to cut and weave in the yarn ends. Yarn needles are specifically made for this purpose and come in a variety of shapes, sizes, and materials. Look for a yarn needle that has a large eye opening, so that you can fit any thickness of yarn through it, and one that has somewhat of a blunt point at its tip so that the needle won't split the yarn.

Scissors: A good pair of strong, small, sharp scissors is important for cutting yarn and thread. Paper scissors certainly work; however, scissors designed for embroidery work are best.

Row counter: This is a handy tracking tool for those who have many things going on in life at any given time. You can twist the dial of a row counter to correspond to the row number you are working on at the time so that if you need to interrupt your crocheting, when you come back to it, you'll know where you left off.

Stitch markers: There are times in patterns when you need to mark certain stitches for later reference. Stitch markers come in handy for this purpose. They come in a variety of shapes and sizes, such as circles, pins, and even hearts. If need be, a paper clip, safety pin, or piece of scrap yarn can also serve to mark a stitch.

Rulers and measuring tapes: Measuring clothing items in broomstick lace is critical. You can get the best fit if you measure both the intended wearer as well as your stitches. Flat school rulers work great for measuring stitches, while flexible measuring tapes are necessary for measuring heads, hips, and more.

Finished Measurements

The final measurements of the pieces are based on working in the gauge listed for each pattern. For some of the designs, I have provided directions for multiple sizes and the measurements for those sizings will all be listed. In the directions, the stitch differences between the sizes are handled as follows, in this example assuming there is a small, medium, and large:

CH 20 (30, 40).

The smallest size is outside of the parentheses, then the additional sizings follow in order inside the parentheses.

Gauge

Gauge in crochet and knitting refers to the measurement of stitches, namely the number of stitches and number of rows per inch of worked fabric.

Below is an example you might find in a pattern:

15 stitches and 14 rows in single crochet = 4"/10 cm square

This means that the final measurements of the particular project are based on 15 stitches worked across in single crochet measuring 4"/10 cm and 15 rows worked in single crochet measuring 4"/10 cm up and down.

Your first step will be to crochet a test swatch using the size hook indicated in the pattern. Why do this? Because not everyone crochets with the same tension. Tension refers to how tightly or loosely you work. By crocheting a test swatch, you are checking your tension against that of the pattern.

Count the number of stitches across one row within 4"/10 cm. There should be 15 stitches.

Next, count the number of rows within 4"/10 cm. There should be 14 rows.

In a perfect world, your test swatch will hit the gauge numbers spot on and you can start the project, knowing your crocheted item will end up the same size as listed in the pattern when completed.

Another example of gauge you will find in this book is:

4 completed broomstick lace clusters and 4 completed broomstick lace cluster rows = 4"/10 cm square

This means that the final measurements of the particular project are based on 4 completed broomstick lace clusters measuring 4"/10 cm and 4 completed broomstick lace rows measuring 4"/10 cm up and down.

Adjusting Gauge

Chances are you will most likely need to make some adjustments in order to achieve the correct gauge.

Going with the first gauge example, if you have less than 15 stitches across the row within the 4"/10 cm and/or you have less than 14 rows within the 4"/10 cm, it means you are crocheting looser than the pattern writer. You can either consciously tighten up your stitches as you crochet or switch to a smaller crochet hook. You may need to try several hook sizes before you find the correct fit. If neither of those options is working, you can try using a slightly thinner yarn or thread.

If you have more than 15 stitches across the row within the 4"/10 cm and/or you have more than 14 rows within the 4"/10 cm, it means you are crocheting tighter than the pattern writer. You can either consciously loosen up your stitches as you crochet or try using a larger crochet hook. You may need to try several hook sizes before you find the correct fit. If neither of those options is working, you can try using a slightly thicker yarn or thread.

In some cases, nothing you do will correct the gauge issue. In these instances, you may need to alter the actual pattern. If the broomstick lace pattern calls for a starting chain of 20, and the loops are taken off in groups of 5, you might need to create a starting chain of 15 instead if your stitches are too large. Or you might need to add stitches and start with a chain of 25 if your stitches are too small.

Use your own judgment as to how critical it is to achieve the exact gauge. A blanket that ends up a few inches longer and wider than the pattern indicated is not something to worry about, but a smartphone cover that ends up being the size of a paperback book is. Each of my patterns will state the gauge needed to achieve the final measurements using the crochet hook size and weight of yarn listed.

Pattern Notes

Before you start a project, please check under Pattern Notes for important information or tips about how the design is worked.

Special Stitches

A few of the patterns include stitches not covered in Basic Stitches. They are noted in Special Stitches, along with how to do them.

Crochet Abbreviations

This book uses American English crochet terminology, not British English.

Abbreviation	Description
CH	chain
cm	centimeter
DC	double crochet
dec	decrease
g	grams
HDC	half double crochet
inc	increase
m	meter
mm	millimeter
oz	ounce
rnd(s)	round(s)
SC	single crochet
SC2TOG	single crochet 2 stitches together
st(s)	stitch(es)
tog	together
yd(s)	yard(s)
YO	yarn over

Repeat between * and *: In order to save space, pattern writers will denote a repeated set of instructions by using an asterisk symbol at both the beginning and ending of a repeated phrase. When you repeat between * and *, you will work the instructions found in between the two asterisk symbols as many times as is indicated in the directions or as many times as needed to complete a row or round.

Rnds v. Rows: When creating items that are circular in shape, patterns will be written and numbered in rounds, e.g., Rnd 1, Rnd 2. When items are created in rectangular shapes using the back-and-forth method, patterns will be written and numbered in Rows, e.g., Row 1, Row 2.

Finishing

Finishing a crocheted item correctly so that all of the work you just completed doesn't unravel or curl up is an extremely important step in the process. Also, nicely finished crochet items look neat and professional.

Weaving in Ends

Once you have completed work on your item, it is time to properly finish it by cutting the yarn strand and weaving in the ends.

1. Using a pair of scissors, cut the yarn 6"/15.2 cm to 12"/30.5 cm away from the last stitch, depending upon how much weaving in of this yarn end you will need to do.

3. Thread the yarn end through a yarn needle. Turn your work to the wrong side, the side that will not be showing when used or worn. You will be making very small stitches to secure the yarn, so it is best to make these stitches on the side of your work that no one will see, if possible.

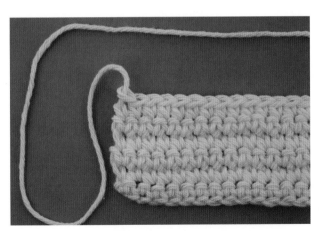

2. Pull the crochet hook and the loop still on it straight upwards until the yarn strand comes out the top section of the last stitch. This is called fastening off.

4. Taking very small stitches, insert the needle under a strand of yarn or two, and then pull it through. You do not want the needle to go all the way through to the other side of your work.

(continued)

5. Repeat the process several more times. Five or six of these small stitches should be sufficient to secure the end; however, you might need to make more or less stitches based upon the texture of the yarn as well as how much wear and tear the item may receive from the recipient.

7. For those whose ends still come undone no matter how much they weave them in, a small dab of washable fabric glue right at the cut location will help hold things in place permanently; this product is not the same as washable school glue, which will come out when washed.

6. Once your stitches are completed, use your scissors to cut the yarn end relatively close to the work. Repeat this process for the original tail end on your work as well.

Blocking

Blocking refers to the process of properly shaping a finished handmade item by washing or steaming it, then stretching and or pinning it in place and letting it dry. You may want to do this to stretch the piece to its intended finished measurements. Another reason to do it is that a freshly finished piece of crochet or knitting may not look that great: the edges might be rippling or curling up or the piece might be misshapen, not that neat rectangle, square, or triangle shape it should be. Blocking relaxes the fibers so that they can be manipulated and the piece be given proper shape.

There are several ways you can block.

SPRAY BLOCKING

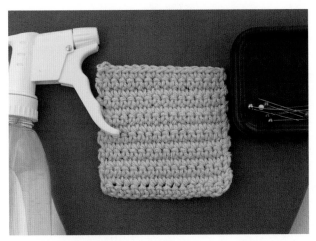

1. You will need a spray bottle filled with cool water, rust-proof pins, and a flat surface that is safe for pinning. An ironing board works well, as do foam play mats found in children's stores. You can also purchase blocking boards from yarn specialty shops.

2. Lay your item flat on the surface and begin to pin your piece to the shape you want. Use as many pins as needed to achieve the correct shape.

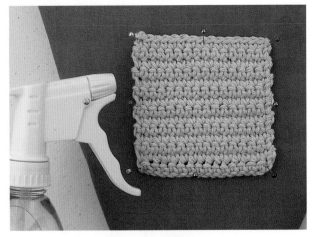

3. Spray the item with water. Some items only need a light spray of water, while others will need a heavy drenching. Let your piece air-dry completely before removing it from the blocking surface.

STEAM BLOCKING

For more stubborn items that are not responding to the spray blocking process, steam might be a better alternative. The preparation process for steam blocking is the same as for shaping with cool water.

Ideally, you will want to use a clothes steamer to produce the steam. However, if you use an iron to produce the steam, never place the iron directly on the crocheted item. Hold it at least 6"/15.2 cm away from your work and then release the steam. If you place a hot iron directly on an item made from yarn, especially acrylic yarn, the yarn could melt and damage the bottom of your iron as well as possibly burn your skin.

You will need to take extra precautions when using steam, as the heat might adversely affect some yarn. Yarn made from plant fibers usually responds nicely to the steam treatment. Natural animal fibers like wool also do well; however, you will want to take care not to move the fibers around during the steam process in order to avoid any possible shrinkage. Man-made fibers like acrylic are extremely sensitive to heat and are known to melt under hot conditions. With steam blocking, always test a very small, inconspicuous spot on your finished item first before proceeding.

OTHER METHODS

Products like fabric stiffener can also be very useful to help the finished item keep its shape, especially if it is an item that will not be worn as clothing, like curtains or a purse.

You will pin the item as for spray blocking, but then spray it with the fabric stiffener as per the instructions on the bottle. Let the product air-dry completely before removing the item from the blocking board.

Infinity Scarf

This is a great project to start with if you're new to broomstick lace. It works up quickly in back-and-forth rows and is then sewn together to create the loop. If you like, you can omit that step and wear it as a regular long scarf. Feel free to add fringe!

You can tailor this scarf to your climate. For warmer areas, work it up in a lightweight 100% cotton or bamboo yarn. If you live in a colder climate, 100% wool (or a wool blend) or other animal fiber like alpaca will be a cozier choice. For a year-round scarf, an acrylic or acrylic blend may work best.

You can opt for a solid-color yarn or a self-striping yarn with relatively slow color changes; one with rapid color shifts will detract from the lovely curves of the broomstick lace stitch. Crochet some swatches and see what works best for you.

SIZES
Small (Large)

YARN
150 yd/138 m (300 yd/276 m) medium worsted #4 weight
    yarn (shown here in Lily® Sugar 'n Cream® Stripes, #21143
    Country Stripes, 100% cotton; 95 yd/86 m, 2 oz/57 g
    per skein)

OTHER MATERIALS
- U.S. size H-8 (5 mm) crochet hook, or size needed to
  obtain gauge
- U.S. size 35 (19 mm) knitting needle or broomstick lace
  pin 10"/25.5 cm or 14"/35.5 cm long
- Yarn needle
- Scissors

GAUGE
4 complete broomstick lace clusters x 3 rows completed
    broomstick lace clusters (6 rows total) = 4"/10 cm square
*Gauge isn't crucial to this project since the scarf is meant to be
    worn long or wrapped around your neck.*

FINISHED MEASUREMENTS
Small: 4"/10 cm wide, 63"/160 cm long
Large: 8"/20 cm wide, 63"/160 cm long

Notes

- In this pattern, the broomstick lace is worked in single crochet in clusters of 4 loops.
- You can also change the length of the scarf to your liking by increasing or decreasing the number of rows. Always finish with Row 2.
- If you want to change the width of the scarf, increase or decrease the number of starting chains by multiples of four.
- The scarf shown in the photos is the smaller size.

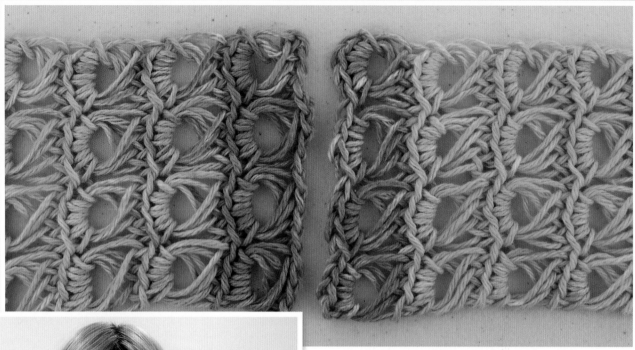

The two ends of the scarf, lined up to be sewn together. If you prefer, don't sew the ends together and instead wear it as a long scarf.

Scarf

CH 16 (32).

Row 1: Slip the loop from the crochet hook to the knitting needle, then YO through the back loop of each chain, pulling the resultant loop onto the needle. At the end of the row, you should have 16 (32) loops.

Row 2: Insert the hook through the first 4 loops, YO, pull through, and CH 1. Slip the loops off the needle. Make 4 SC in the middle of them. *Slip the next 4 loops off the needle. Make 4 SC in the middle of them.* Repeat between * and * across the entire row. At the end of the row, you will have completed 4 (8) broomstick lace clusters.

Row 3: YO through the back loop of each SC, pulling the resultant loop onto the needle. At the end of the row, you should have 16 (32) loops.

Row 4: Repeat Row 2.

Rows 5–94: Repeat Rows 3 and 4.

Cut the yarn, leaving an 18"/45.7 cm tail.

Finishing

Fold the scarf in half so the short ends line up with one another. With the yarn needle, sew the two ends together using a whipstitch or other comparable stitch. Cut and weave in all ends.

Pretty
in Pink
Pillow
Cover

47

This pillow cover combines the delicate look of broomstick lace with the durability of super bulky weight yarn for a finished item that will last even with everyday use. It is crocheted as a single rectangular piece that is sewn together up the sides. The flap is held closed by ribbon or buttons that easily fit through the broomstick lace clusters. Buttons, especially, allow for easy removal of the cover for laundering.

Notes

- Review the tutorial Changing Colors in Broomstick Lace (page 23).
- If you prefer, you can crochet the entire pillow cover in a single color; you'll need 300 yd/274 m.
- The broomstick lace pattern is worked in single crochet (SC) in clusters of 4 loops.

Most craft and sewing stores sell plain pillow forms; however, you can sew your own with fabric in a matching or contrasting color and use polyester fiberfill as a stuffing material.

YARN
Color A: 150 yd/137 m super bulky #6 weight yarn (shown in Lion Brand® Wool-Ease® Thick & Quick®, #103 Blossom, 80% acrylic, 20% wool; 106 yd/97 m, 6 oz/170 g per skein)
Color B: 150 yd/137 m super bulky #6 weight yarn (shown in Lion Brand® Wool-Ease® Thick & Quick®, #099 Fisherman, 80% acrylic, 20% wool; 106 yd/97 m, 6 oz/170 g per skein)

OTHER MATERIALS
- U.S. size N-15 (9 or 10 mm, depending on the brand) crochet hook, or size needed to obtain gauge
- U.S. size 35 (19 mm) knitting needle or broomstick lace pin, 14"/35.5 cm long
- Yarn needle
- Scissors
- 16"/40 cm square pillow form
- Decorative ribbon 1"/2.5 cm wide or several matching buttons
- Clip-on ribbon flower (optional)

GAUGE
4 completed broomstick lace clusters x 4 rows completed broomstick lace clusters (8 rows total) = 6"/15.2 cm square

Because you want the pillow cover to fit the pillow form snugly—neither too loosely nor too tightly—gauge is important. Some pillow forms have a zipper that allows you to add or remove stuffing material. This can help regulate the size of your pillow if you have a problem getting the right gauge.

FINISHED MEASUREMENTS
16.5"/42 cm square

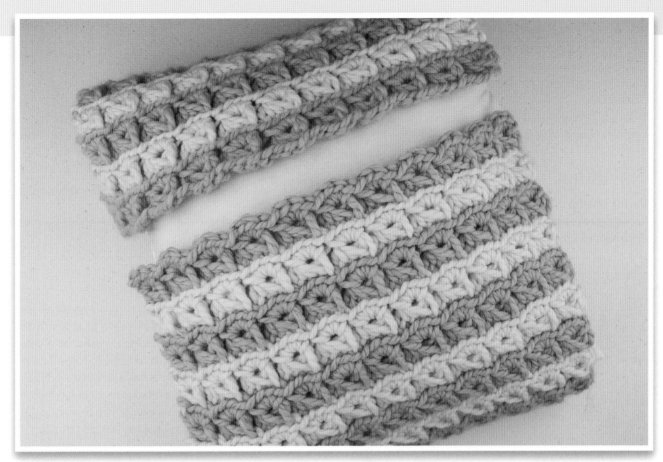

Check the size of the pillow cover against the form periodically; remember, you want the form to fit very snugly inside the cover.

Pillow Cover

With Color A yarn and your crochet hook, CH 44.

Row 1: Slip the loop from the crochet hook onto the knitting needle, then YO through the back loop of each chain, pulling it through and onto the needle. At the end of the row, you should have 44 loops on your needle.

Row 2: Insert the hook through the first 4 loops, YO, pull it through, and CH 1. Slip the loops off the needle. Make 4 SC in the middle of them. *Slip the next 4 loops off the needle. Make 4 SC in the middle of them.* Repeat between * and * until the last set of 4 loops. Slip the loops off the needle, make 3 SC in the middle of them. For the final SC, insert the crochet hook through the loops, YO, and pull through. Drop Color A. With the crochet hook, grab Color B and pull it through the 2 loops remaining on the hook to complete the SC. At the end of this row, you will have completed 11 broomstick lace clusters.

Row 3: YO through the back loop of each SC, pulling it through and up onto the knitting needle. You should have a total of 44 loops.

Row 4: Repeat Row 2, switching colors at the end of the row as directed.

Note how the alternating colors of yarn are carried upwards along the edge of the pillow. Because this is occurring along the back side of your work, you will not see this in the finished pillow.

Rows 5–50: Repeat Rows 3 and 4. Periodically measure your work against your pillow form. You may need to add or subtract rows to get a correct fit; keep in mind that for the pillow to fit properly in the cover, with no looseness or wrinkling of the cover, you might need to push the pillow into the cover to make it fit. The cover should need to stretch a bit to accommodate the pillow for a nice, smooth fit. Also remember that you want the last row of broomstick lace to be the same color as the first row because they will overlap each other to form a small flap.

Once you have achieved a size that properly fits the pillow, cut and weave in all ends.

Finishing

Decide whether you would like your broomstick lace clusters to face up or down on your pillow cover. There is no right or wrong way with broomstick lace.

Broomstick lace clusters facing downward.

Broomstick lace clusters right side up.

With the wrong sides of your work facing outward, fold the piece how you want your finished pillow to appear. You can make the horizontal flap appear near the top of the pillow, a third of the way down, or halfway down. Be sure to fold it so that the first row of broomstick lace overlaps the last row. Pin the edges in place if needed and then sew the edges together with a whipstitch or other comparable stitch using a matching yarn and the yarn needle. Leave the horizontal flap part unsewn.

Turn the pillow cover right side out and insert the pillow form, which will require really packing it into the cover.

Pin the edges together with the wrong sides facing out.

The pillow form needs to be very tightly packed inside the cover; if the cover is too big, the form will be jiggling and wiggling loosely around inside and the outside cover will be wrinkled.

If all looks correct, you have several choices. You can enjoy your pillow as is, since the flap will stay closed. You can weave a decorative ribbon through the broomstick lace clusters so it grabs both the top and bottom layers of the flap to more securely close the flap. Add a clip-on ribbon flower for an added touch. Or sew buttons on the bottom layer of the flap and use the holes formed by the broomstick lace clusters as buttonholes.

If you need to launder the cover, remove the flower and ribbon if you've added them, then the pillow form. Unless you've used an acrylic yarn, I would hand wash the cover to prevent any shrinkage.

The cover with buttons sewn on.

The cover with a ribbon woven through the flap.

Boot Cuffs

oot cuffs look great peeking over the top of your boots, and they are super quick to work up. Make multiple pairs using different colored yarns and/or customize them as you like with the addition of buttons, ribbons, flowers, or bows.

SIZES
Small (Medium, Large)

YARN
150 yd/137.25 m (200 yd/183 m, 250 yd/229 m) medium worsted #4 weight yarn (shown in Lion Brand® Vanna's Choice®, #123 Beige, 100% acrylic; 170 yd/156 m, 3.5 oz/100 g per skein)

OTHER MATERIALS
- U.S. size H-8 (5 mm) crochet hook, or size needed to obtain gauge
- U.S. size 19 (15 mm) knitting needle or broomstick lace pin, 14"/35.5 cm long
- Yarn needle
- Scissors
- Flowers, ties, ribbon, buttons, snaps, or other fasteners (optional)

GAUGE
15 stitches x 14 rows in single crochet = 4"/10 cm square
Gauge isn't crucial to this pattern since the cuffs are tucked into your boot tops, but it will affect how loose or tight a fit they are on your calf.

FINISHED MEASUREMENTS
Measured before seaming.
Small: 14.5"/37 cm x 8"/20 cm
Medium: 16"/41 cm x 8"/20 cm
Large: 18"/45.7 cm x 8"/20 cm
The small size is recommended if the cuff will be worn with shorter boots that extend just above the ankle. For those who wear taller boots, medium or large will likely be a better choice, and large definitely for thigh-high boots.

Notes

- The body of the cuff is worked single crochet (SC), then edged along one long side in broomstick lace. Clusters of 5 SC are worked first into groups of 4 loops and then into groups of 5 loops so that the top of the cuff will flair slightly.
- The cuffs are worked flat, then the ends are seamed together.
- To customize the fit, you can increase or decrease the number of single crochet rows, as long as it is a multiple of four. Keep in mind that the cuffs will stretch. You can also increase or decrease the width of the broomstick lace edging as suits you.

Boot Cuff (make 2)

Base of Boot Cuff

With your crochet hook, CH 16 (16, 16).

Row 1: Skip the first chain, make 1 SC in the next chain and each chain across. You will have a total of 15 (15, 15) SC once completed. CH 1 and turn your work.

Row 2: Skip the CH 1, using back loops only, make 1 SC in the next stitch and each stitch across. CH 1 and turn your work.

Repeat Row 2 46 (54, 62) times.

Broomstick Lace Edging

You will work the edging along one of the long sides, using the ends of the row as base stitches for Row 1. Slip the loop from the crochet hook to the knitting needle.

Row 1: YO through the end of each row, pulling the loop through and onto the needle. At the end of the row, the number of loops on the needle should match the number of SC rows: 48 (56, 64) loops. If you had added or subtracted SC rows, the number of loops should equal that number.

Row 2: Insert the hook through the first 4 loops, YO, pull through, and CH 1. Slip the loops off the needle. Make 5 SC in the middle of them. *Slip the next 4 loops off the needle. Make 5 SC in the middle of them.* Repeat between * and * across the entire row. At the end of this row, you will have completed 12 (14, 16) broomstick lace clusters.

Row 3: Repeat the process from Row 1, drawing up loops using the back loops only of the SC stitches. You should have 60 (70, 80) loops on your needle.

Row 4: Insert the hook through the first 5 loops, YO, pull through, and CH 1. Slip the loops off the needle. Make 5 SC in the middle of them. *Slip the next 5 loops off the needle. Make 5 SC in the middle of them.* Repeat between * and * across the entire row. At the end of this row, you will have completed 12 (14, 16) broomstick lace clusters.

Rows 5–8: Repeat Rows 3 and 4.

Cut the yarn, leaving an 18"/46 cm to 24"/60 cm tail for sewing the seam.

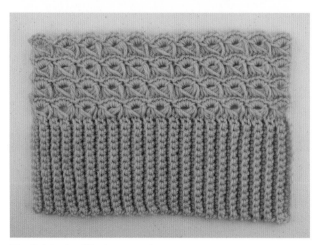

The finished cuff before seaming.

Finishing

Place the two short sides of the cuff together. Thread the yarn needle with the yarn tail, then, using a whipstitch or other comparable stitch, sew the two ends together. You can choose to sew the entire seam or just the single crochet sections together.

The finished cuff after seaming. I've left it open at the broomstick edging, but you can seam it all the way up, if you prefer.

If you leave the broomstick lace section open, buttons or other fasteners can be used to close the opening. The holes produced by the broomstick lace clusters can serve as buttonholes for the buttons. Once completed, cut and weave in all ends.

If you sew the entire seam, you can attach a flower or bow in place of the buttons. Another option is to weave ribbon in and out of the first row of broomstick lace clusters.

You can add buttons anywhere you like or leave them off entirely. Positioned in this way, the broomstick clusters on the other side can be used as buttonholes.

Tote Bag

Crocheted using super bulky weight yarn, this tote works up very quickly. The yarn also makes the tote strong and sturdy, while still showing off the broomstick lace stitch.

YARN

Color A: 150 yd/137 m super bulky #6 weight yarn (shown in Lion Brand® Wool-Ease® Thick & Quick®, #099 Fisherman, hand dyed dark pink, 80% acrylic, 20% wool; 106 yd/97 m, 6 oz/170 g per skein)

Color B: 120 yd/110 m super bulky #6 weight yarn (shown in Lion Brand® Wool-Ease® Thick & Quick®, #099 Fisherman, hand dyed orange, 80% acrylic, 20% wool; 106 yd/97 m, 6 oz/170 g per skein)

Color C: 60 yd/55 m super bulky #6 weight yarn (shown in Lion Brand® Wool-Ease® Thick & Quick®, #099 Fisherman, hand dyed yellow, 80% acrylic, 20% wool; 106 yd/97 m, 6 oz/170 g per skein)

OTHER MATERIALS

- U.S. size N-15 (9 or 10 mm, depending on the brand) crochet hook, or size needed to obtain gauge
- 2 U.S. size 35 (19 mm) knitting needles or broomstick lace pins, 14"/35.5 cm long, or 1 circular knitting needle, 29"/74 cm long
- Yarn needle
- Scissors
- Sew-on tote handles or thick rope to create your own tote handles
- Button, zipper, or other closures for the top (optional)
- Embellishments such as flowers, bows, beads, or ribbon (optional)

GAUGE

3 completed broomstick lace clusters x 3 rows completed broomstick lace clusters (6 rows total) = 4"/10 cm square

Gauge is not critical to this project unless you want it to match the finished measurements given here.

FINISHED MEASUREMENTS

14"/35.5 cm square

SPECIAL STITCHES

Reverse slip stitch: This stitch is like a traditional slip stitch, except the stitch is made in the opposite direction. Insert your hook under the designated stitch, yarn over, and pull it through all loops on your hook.

Notes

- The tote is worked in a single piece in the round from the bottom up—no need for any seams! The combined weight of the needle and yarn is somewhat heavy, so I recommend you take periodic breaks to avoid straining your wrist or arms.
- The broomstick lace pattern is worked in single crochet (SC) in clusters of four.
- Review the tutorial Changing Colors in Broomstick Lace (page 23); at the color switch, the dropped yarn should be cut.
- Review the tutorial Broomstick Lace in the Round (page 30).
- Believe it or not, I hand dyed the yarn using different flavors of Kool-Aid!
- Feel free to make the tote using yarn all of one color or to change the width of the stripes and the number of colors used.

You will draw up 40 loops onto each knitting needle, with the starting chain running down the middle of them.

Tote

With your crochet hook and Color A, CH 40. This will be referred to as the starting chain.

Rnd 1a: Slip the loop from the crochet hook onto one of the knitting needles, then YO through the back loop of each chain, pulling it through and onto the needle. At the end of the rnd, you should have 40 loops.

Rnd 1b: Pivot your work so that you are working on the opposite side of the starting chain. YO through the back loop of each chain, pulling it through and onto the second knitting needle. You should have 40 loops on the second knitting needle.

Rnd 2: Insert the hook through the first 4 loops, YO, pull it through, and CH 1. Slip the loops off the needle. Make 4 SC in the middle of them. *Slip the next 4 loops off the needle. Make 4 SC in the middle of them.* Repeat between * and * across both knitting needles. At the end of the rnd, you will have completed 20 broomstick lace clusters. Make a slip stitch to the first SC to join the rnd.

Rnd 3: Make a reverse slip stitch into the last SC made from the previous rnd. Slip the loop from the crochet hook onto one of the knitting needles, then YO through the back loop of each SC, pulling it through and onto the needle. Once the first 40 loops have been pulled up onto the first needle, pivot your work and continue drawing up loops onto the second knitting needle. Once completed, you will have a total of 80 loops, with 40 loops on each needle.

Rnd 4: Repeat Rnd 2.

Rnds 5–10: Repeat Rnds 3 and 2 three times; for the last slip stitch of Rnd 10, insert the crochet hook through the stitch and drop Color A. With the crochet hook, grab Color B and pull it through both loops to complete the slip stitch. Cut Color A.

Rnds 11–18: Repeat Rnds 3 and 2 four times; for the last slip stitch of Rnd 18, insert the crochet hook through the stitch and drop Color B. With the crochet hook, grab Color C and pull it through both loops to complete the slip stitch. Cut Color B.

Rnds 19–22: Repeat Rnds 3 and 2 two times.

Cut yarn and weave in all ends.

Finishing

Once your tote is crocheted, add purchased or handmade handles. Many purse handles are sewn on using a matching yarn and yarn needle; refer to the instructions that came with your handles for proper placement. If you like, you can sew a zipper to secure the opening at the top or add a button or other fastener. Decorative elements such as ribbon can be woven around the tote through the holes produced by the broomstick cluster stitches.

Sew or glue on bows, buttons, flowers, or other embellishments if you choose.

If your yarn is stiff enough, you might not need to line the purse. If you feel one is necessary, see page 74 for directions on how to make a quick and easy lining.

Baby
Sweater

See page 63 for the pattern for the matching hat.

This pretty baby sweater makes a wonderful "Welcome, baby!" gift. The body is worked in single crochet, with the arms and yoke worked in broomstick lace.

Notes

- The broomstick lace pattern is worked in single crochet (SC) in clusters of 4 loops.
- The sweater is worked in two pieces, from the bottom up, then sewn together.
- The yoke and sleeves are created in one piece by increasing the body section via chains on both sides.

SIZES
0–6 months (6–12 months, 12–18 months)

YARN
175 yd/160 m (200 yd/183 m, 225 yd/205.75 m) medium worsted #4 weight yarn (shown in Caron® Simply Soft®, #9719 Soft Pink, 100% acrylic; 315 yd/288 m, 6 oz/170 g per skein)

OTHER MATERIALS
- U.S. size G-6 (4 or 4.25 mm, depending on the brand) crochet hook, or size needed to obtain gauge
- U.S. size 19 (16 mm) knitting needle or broomstick lace pin, 14"/35.5 cm long
- Yarn needle
- Scissors
- Accessory like a bow or flower (optional). If you do choose to include, make sure it is not something that can easily come off the sweater and pose a choking risk to the baby.

GAUGE
12 stitches x 15 rows in single crochet = 3"/7.6 cm square
For proper fit, gauge is important for this sweater.

FINISHED MEASUREMENTS
Sweater width is the finished sweater, measured flat; length is measured from top of neck to bottom edge.
0–6 months: Width, 8"/20 cm; length, 9"/23 cm
6–12 months: Width, 9"/23 cm; length, 10"/25.5 cm
12–18 months: Width, 10"/25.5 cm; length, 11"/28 cm

Sweater Panels (make 2)

Lower Section

With the crochet hook, CH 33 (37, 41).

Row 1: Skip the first chain. Make 1 SC in the next chain and each chain across. At the end of the row, you will have made 32 (36, 40) SC. CH 1 and turn your work.

Row 2: Skip the chain. Make 1 SC in the next stitch and each stitch across. CH 1 and turn your work.

Repeat Row 2 until you have completed 30 (33, 35) rows. CH 20 (24, 28). Cut the yarn. You will use these chains to work one of the sleeves.

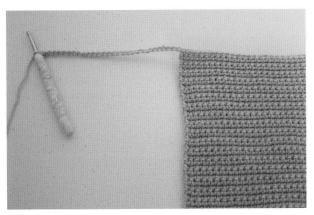

This chain is the foundation row for one of the sleeves.

Join the yarn to the opposite side of the sweater and CH 20 (24, 28). You will work these chains to make the other sleeve. Turn the work and slip the loop on the crochet hook onto the knitting needle.

For the other sleeve, the yarn is joined on the other side of the body, then the chain is worked.

Broomstick Lace Section

Row 1: YO through the back loop of each chain, pulling it through and onto the needle, then do the same through the tops of the SC, then the chains for the other sleeve. At the end of the row you should have 72 (84, 96) loops.

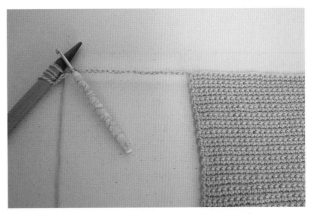

Drawing up loops from one sleeve's chain.

Row 2: Insert the crochet hook through the first 4 loops on the needle, YO, pull it through, and CH 1. Slip the loops off the needle. Make 4 SC in the middle of them. *Slip the next 4 loops off the needle. Make 4 SC in the middle of them.* Repeat between * and * across the entire row. At the end of the row, you will have completed 18 (21, 24) broomstick lace clusters.

Row 3: YO through the back loop of each SC, pulling it through and up onto the knitting needle.

Row 4: Repeat Row 2.

Completed front and back pieces.

Repeat Rows 3 and 4 until you have 6 (8, 10) rows total. Cut the yarn and leave a long tail for sewing.

Finishing

After you have completed the two pieces, place them on top of one another to sew the seams. Depending upon your sewing style, you can place either the wrong sides together or the right sides together.

Whatever method you choose, use a whipstitch or other comparable stitch to seam the front and back pieces together, then cut the yarn and weave in the ends.

You can add decorative items such as a ribbon, flower, or bow to the sweater, but take care to ensure that the item is very firmly secured to the sweater and does not pose a choking hazard to the baby.

Align the pieces to sew together, making sure that either both wrong sides or both right sides are facing, depending on your preferred sewing method.

Baby Hat

This adorable broomstick lace–edged hat works up very quickly in single crochet. Although I used only one color yarn, you could crochet the hat in two colors, using one for the base of the hat and another for the broomstick lace edging.

Notes

- The hat is worked back and forth in rows, then seamed together in the back.
- The broomstick lace pattern is worked as edging along the ends of the rows of one long side of the rectangular piece. It's worked in single crochet, with the number of SC and the number of loops in each cluster increasing on each row, which causes the edging to flare out attractively.

SIZES
0–6 months (6–12 months, 12–18 months)

YARN
125 yd/114 m (150 yd/137 m, 175 yd/160 m) medium worsted #4 weight yarn (shown in Caron® Simply Soft®, #9719 Soft Pink, 100% acrylic; 315 yd/288 m, 6 oz/170 g per skein)

OTHER MATERIALS
- U.S. size G-6 (4 or 4.25 mm, depending on the brand) crochet hook, or size needed to obtain gauge
- U.S. size 19 (16 mm) knitting needle or broomstick lace pin, 14"/35.5 cm long
- Yarn needle
- Scissors
- Bow, ribbon, or flower as decoration (optional). If you do add this kind of ornamentation, make sure it is firmly secured to the hat and not something the baby could choke on.

GAUGE
12 stitches x 12 rows in single crochet = 3"/7.6 cm square
For proper fit, gauge is important for this hat.

FINISHED MEASUREMENTS
0–6 months: Circumference, 14"/35.5 cm; height, 5"/12.7 cm
6–12 months: Circumference, 16"/40.6 cm; height, 6"/15.2 cm
12–18 months: Circumference, 18"/45.7 cm; height, 7"/17.8 cm

Hat

Body of Hat

With the crochet hook, CH 13 (17, 21).

Row 1: Skip the first chain. Make 1 SC in the next chain and each across. At the end of the row, you will have made 12 (16, 20) SC. CH 1 and turn your work.

Row 2: Skip the chain. Make 1 SC in the next stitch and each stitch across. CH 1 and turn your work.

Repeat Row 2 until you have completed a total of 56 (64, 72) rows. Measure your work once completed, and use the Finished Measurements to check that it is the correct circumference. For example, if you are making the 0–6 month size, the longest side of the rectangle should be 14"/35.5 cm. If the hat is too small, add rows in groups of four. If the hat is too large, subtract rows by pulling them out in groups of four. It is important for the broomstick lace edging that the number of total rows you make for this part of the hat is divisible by four.

Broomstick Lace Edging

You will work the broomstick lace edging along one of the long sides of the rectangular piece. If you are right-handed, the last SC loop should be on your left. If you are left-handed, the loop should be on your right. Slip the loop from your crochet hook to your knitting needle.

Row 1: Working the ends of the SC rows as stitches, YO through each stitch, pulling the loop through and up onto the knitting needle. You should have 56 (64, 72) loops. If you added or subtracted single crochet rows, the number of loops on your knitting needle should equal the number of rows of single crochet.

Drawing up the loops and placing them on the knitting needle for Row 3 of the edging.

Row 2: Insert the crochet hook through the first 4 loops on the needle, YO, pull it through, and CH 1. Slip the loops off the needle. Make 5 SC in the middle of them. *Slip the next 4 loops off the needle. Make 5 SC in the middle of them.* Repeat between * and * across the entire row. At the end of the row, you will have completed 14 (16, 18) broomstick lace clusters.

Row 3: YO through the back loop only of each SC, pulling it through and up onto the knitting needle. You should have 70 (80, 90) loops.

Row 4: Insert the crochet hook through the first 5 loops on the needle, YO, pull it through, and CH 1. Slip the loops off the needle. Make 6 SC in the middle of them. *Slip the next 5 loops off the needle. Make 6 SC in the middle of them.* Repeat between * and * across the row. At the end of the row, you will have completed 14 (16, 18) broomstick lace clusters.

Row 5: YO through the back loop only of each SC, pulling it through and up onto the knitting needle. You should have 84 (96, 108) loops.

Row 6: Insert the crochet hook through the first 6 loops on the needle, YO, pull it through, and CH 1. Slip the loops off the needle. Make 7 SC in the middle of them. *Slip the next 6 loops off the needle. Make 7 SC in the middle of them.* Repeat between * and * across the row. At the end of the row, you will have completed 14 (16, 18) broomstick lace clusters.

Cut the yarn, leaving a 24"/61 cm tail for sewing the back seam of the hat.

The completed broomstick edging; see how the ends flare out because of the increase in stitches on every other row.

Finishing

With the yarn needle, use the tail to whipstitch (or use another comparable stitch) the two short ends together. Start at the bottom edge of the hat and work your way to the top.

At the crown of the hat, take the needle and weave it in and out of the stitches all along the top edge. For a more secure fit, go around twice. Pull the yarn tightly to close up the top of the hat. Securely knot this strand in place. Cut and weave in all ends.

If you want to add a decorative item to the hat, please ensure it is attached securely. If the hat will be laundered frequently, a removable hair bow works nicely as a decorative item. You can easily insert this within the spaces formed by the broomstick lace clusters.

To close the top of the hat, weave the yarn needle in and out of the stitches all the way around, then pull tightly to cinch the opening closed.

Cutie Booties

These sweet little tootsie toasters are a little more sock than booty, which means there is a greater likelihood that they will stay put on baby's feet! The booties are worked in single crochet, with a decorative ankle cuff of broomstick lace added afterward. Crochet a rainbow set of them so baby has matching socks no matter what she's wearing!

Notes

- Each booty is worked in rows of single crochet down to the beginning of the instep; from that point, it is worked in the round. The toe is closed by weaving the yarn in and out of the stitches and then cinching the opening shut. The broomstick edging is added to the other end of the booty, working the ends of the single crochet rows as stitches to pick up the loops. The edging is worked in rounds. See the tutorial for Broomstick Lace in the Round on page 30.
- The broomstick lace pattern is worked in single crochet (SC) in clusters of 3 loops.

SIZES
0–6 months (6–12 months)

YARN
150 yd/137 m fine #2 or DK #3 weight yarn (shown in Premier® Cotton Fair®, #2705 Baby Pink, 52% cotton, 48% acrylic; 317 yd/ 290 m, 3.5 oz/100 g per skein)

OTHER MATERIALS
- U.S. size E-4 (3.5 mm) crochet hook, or size needed to obtain gauge
- 2 or 3 U.S. size 15 (10 mm) knitting needles or broomstick lace pins, 10"/25.5 cm long
- Yarn needle
- Stitch marker or scrap piece of yarn
- Scissors
- Decorative ribbon, bow, or flower (optional). Please ensure these items are firmly secured to the booties to avoid any possible choking hazard for the baby.

GAUGE
14 stitches x 14 rows in single crochet= 3"/7.6 cm square
For proper fit, gauge is important for these baby booties.

FINISHED MEASUREMENTS
0–6 months: Sole length, 3.75"/9.5 cm; height of bootie, 3"/7.6 cm
6–12 months: Sole length, 4.5"/11.4 cm; height of bootie, 3.5"/8.9 cm

SPECIAL STITCHES
SC2TOG (single crochet 2 together): This is a decrease stitch. Insert your crochet hook under the front loop of the indicated stitch, then insert the hook under the front loop of the next stitch—you now have 3 loops on your hook. Yarn over and pull through the first 2 loops on the hook. Yarn over and pull through the remaining two loops on your hook.
Reverse slip stitch: This stitch is like regular slip stitch, except it is made in the opposite direction. Insert your hook under the designated stitch, yarn over, and pull through all the loops on your hook.

Booties (make 2)

Heel Section

With the crochet hook, CH 10 (13).

Row 1a: Skip the first chain. Make 1 SC in the next chain and each across. At the end of the row, you will have made 9 (12) SC.

Row 1b: Pivot your work so that you are working along the other side of the starting chain. Make 1 SC on the other side of the same chain that you completed your last SC stitch from Row 1a. Make 1 SC in the next chain and each chain across. At the end of the row, you will have made 9 (12) SC. CH 1 and turn your work.

You will begin working in rows that have somewhat of a U shape to them, as opposed to traditional straight-line rows.

Row 2: Skip the first CH. *Make 1 SC in the next stitch and each stitch across. At the end of this U-shaped row, you will have made 18 (24) SC. CH 1 and turn your work.

Repeat Row 2 for a total of 12 (15) rows. After completing the last row, do not CH 1 and do not turn your work.

Toe Section

0–6 Months

At this point, you will be working in rounds instead of rows.

Rnd 1: Reach over to the beginning stitch of the row just completed and make 1 SC. Place a marker in this stitch to designate it as the first stitch of the rnd. Make 1 SC in the next stitch and each stitch around. At the end of this rnd, right before the stitch marker, you will have 18 SC.

Rnds 2–4: Remove the stitch marker and make 1 SC in that stitch. Place the stitch marker in the SC you just made. Make 1 SC in the next stitch and each stitch around.

Rnd 5: Remove the stitch marker. Make 1 SC2TOG over the next 2 stitches. Place the stitch marker in the stitch you just made. *Make 1 SC in the next stitch. Make 1 SC2TOG over the next 2 stitches.* Repeat from * to * around. At the end of this rnd, you will have a total of 12 SC.

Rnd 6: Remove the stitch marker. Make 1 SC2TOG over the next 2 stitches. Place the stitch marker in the stitch you just made. *Make 1 SC2TOG over the next 2 stitches.* Repeat from * to * around. At the end of this rnd, you will have a total of 6 SC.

6–12 Months

Rnd 1: Reach over to the beginning stitch of the row just completed and make 1 SC. Place a marker in this stitch to designate it as the first stitch of the rnd. Make 1 SC in the next stitch and each stitch around. At the end of this rnd, right before the stitch marker, you will have 24 SC.

Rnds 2–5: Remove the stitch marker and make 1 SC in that stitch. Place the stitch marker in the SC you just made. Make 1 SC in the next stitch and each stitch around.

Rnd 6: Remove the stitch marker. Make 1 SC2TOG over the next 2 stitches. Place the stitch marker in the stitch you just made. *Make 1 SC in the next 2 stitches. Make 1 SC2TOG over the next 2 stitches.* Repeat from * to * around. At the end of this rnd, you will have a total of 18 SC.

Rnd 7: Remove the stitch marker. Make 1 SC2TOG over the next 2 stitches. Place the stitch marker in the stitch you just made. *Make 1 SC in the next stitch. Make 1 SC2TOG over the next 2 stitches.* Repeat from * to * around. At the end of this rnd, you will have a total of 12 SC.

Rnd 8: Remove the stitch marker. Make 1 SC2TOG over the next 2 stitches. Place the stitch marker in the stitch you just made. *Make 1 SC2TOG over the next 2 stitches.* Repeat from * to * around. At the end of this rnd, you will have a total of 6 SC.

Closing the Toe (for both sizes)

Cut the yarn, leaving an 18"/45.7 cm tail. With a yarn needle, use this strand to weave around and close up the tip of the toe section. Knot securely, then cut and weave in all ends.

Broomstick Lace Edging (for both sizes)

Rnd 1: Join the yarn along the back edge of the bootie, preferably at the top of the starting chain. Working the ends of the SC rows as stitches, YO through each stitch, pulling the loop through and up onto the knitting needle. Use as many knitting needles as comfortable for holding these loops. You should have 24 (30) loops on your needles.

Rnd 2: Insert the crochet hook through the first 3 loops on the needle, YO, pull it through, and CH 1. Slip the loops off the needle. Make 3 SC in the middle of them. *Slip the next 3 loops off the needle. Make 3 SC in the middle of them.* Repeat between * and * across the entire rnd. At the end of this rnd, you will have completed a total of 8 (10) broomstick lace clusters. Reach over to the first stitch of the first broomstick lace cluster and make 1 slip stitch. Make a reverse slip stitch back into the last SC completed.

Rnd 3: YO through the back loop only of each SC, pulling it through and up onto the knitting needle. Use as many knitting needles as you need to feel comfortable holding these loops.

Rnd 4: Repeat Rnd 2. Eliminate the reverse slip stitch. Cut and weave in all ends.

Finishing

If you wish, you can weave a decorative ribbon through the broomstick lace edging or firmly sew on decorative bows, flowers, or buttons. If the baby is apt to pull small objects off and place them in his or her mouth, it is best to leave such things off and let the beauty of the broomstick lace stitch become the focal point of these booties.

Evening Bag

This elegant purse is crocheted in single and half double crochet and finished with a decorative broomstick lace flap.

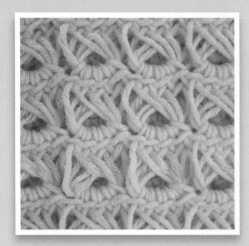

Notes

- Pick a yarn with a certain degree of stiffness to it; this will help give the purse form. If you crochet it in a soft worsted yarn, the purse will end up being floppy. The directions are for working it in a single color but you can change colors and add stripes for a bold effect. Another option is to crochet the body of the purse in one color and its broomstick lace flap in another.

- The purse is crocheted in a single piece and then partially folded over and seamed on both sides.

- The broomstick lace pattern is worked in single crochet (SC) in clusters of 4 loops.

- If when you start to work the broomstick edging it looks like it is crocheting up tighter than the purse SC/HDC pattern, change to a larger crochet hook, such as a size H (5 mm) or as large as needed, so that the broomstick lace doesn't pull inward.

You can use the purse as a hand clutch or add a handle or shoulder strap. For the purse shown here, I added a strong beaded chain that I bought in the jewelry-making section of my local craft store. You can also embellish your purse, if you like, with a bow or flower. To secure the flap, you can sew on a button or use a magnetic purse snap or some other type of closure. You may want to sew in a zipper along the opening to hold in the contents. Also, I have included directions on how to make a simple lining, which you can use for this purse or the tote on page 56—it's entirely optional.

YARN
300 yd/274.5 m medium worsted #4 weight yarn (shown in Patons Classic Wool Worsted, #0202 Aran, 100% wool; 210 yd/192 m, 3.5 oz/100 g per skein)

OTHER MATERIALS
- U.S. size G-6 (4.0 or 4.25 mm, depending on the brand) crochet hook, or size needed to obtain gauge
- U.S. size H (5 mm) or larger crochet hook (optional)
- U.S. size 35 (19 mm) knitting needle or broomstick lace pin, 14"/35.5 cm long
- Yarn needle
- Scissors
- Button for closure (optional)
- Decorative or functional accessories such as bows, flowers, zipper, purse handle, purse strap (optional)

GAUGE
16 stitches x 16 rows purse pattern (single crochet/half-double crochet) = 4"/10 cm square
4 completed broomstick lace clusters x 4 rows completed broomstick lace clusters (8 rows total) = 4"/10 cm square
Gauge is less important for this project unless you want to achieve exactly the same dimensions.

FINISHED MEASUREMENTS
12"/30.5 cm wide, 9"/23 cm high

Purse

Single/Half Double Crochet Section

With your crochet hook, CH 53.

Row 1: Skip the first chain. *SC in the next chain, HDC in the next chain.* Repeat between * and * across the row. At the end of the row, you will have completed 52 stitches. CH 1 and turn your work.

Row 2: Skip the first chain. *SC in the next stitch, under both loops. HDC in the next stitch, again under both loops.* Repeat between * and * across the row. CH 1 and turn your work.

Rows 3–64: Repeat Row 2. If you prefer a deeper purse, you can continue making more rows beyond the suggested 64 rows. At the end of your very last row, do not CH 1.

Broomstick Lace Flap Section

Row 1: Slip the loop from the crochet hook onto the knitting needle, then YO through the back loops only of each SC and HDC across the row, pulling it through and onto the needle. At the end of the row, you should have 52 loops.

Row 2: Insert the hook through the first 4 loops, YO, pull it through, and CH 1. Slip the loops off the needle. Make 4 SC in the middle of them. *Slip the next 4 loops off the needle. Make 4 SC in the middle of them.* Repeat between * and * across the entire row. At the end of the row, you will have completed 13 broomstick lace clusters.

Rows 3–12: Repeat Rows 1 and 2.

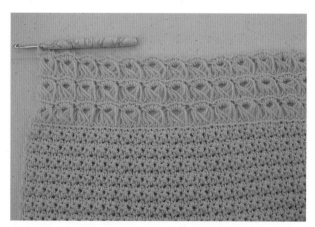

Working the broomstick lace flap section.

Feel free to alter the number of rows in the flap to your liking. You may wish to make the flap smaller or have the flap much longer, touching the bottom of the purse.

Cut the yarn and weave in all the ends. If you plan to use this purse a lot, you may want to consider adding a drop of fabric glue on your secured ends to ensure the yarn does not unravel.

Finishing

Lay the piece on the table, wrong side facing you, with the broomstick lace flap away from you. Fold the bottom of the purse upwards so that the first row of SC/HDC is right below the first row of broomstick lace. Fold the broomstick lace flap over the purse to ensure it fits properly and looks good. Make adjustments as needed with your folding. Once you are satisfied with the folds, thread a yarn needle with an 18" to 24"/45.7 to 61 cm strand of yarn and sew along the purse's two edges, using whipstitch or other comparable stitch. You may want to turn the purse inside out prior to sewing the edges to avoid any visible stitches on the outside; however, this is not a mandatory step. Cut and securely weave in all ends.

Sew a button or other closure on. If you'd like to add a lining, do it now (see below)

Finally, sew on handles or a purse strap if you wish.

Adding a Lining (optional)

If your yarn is stiff enough, you might not need one, but if you do, the process is simple.

Purchase a large piece of craft felt or fleece fabric the same color as your purse. Larger pieces of craft felt can be found in craft stores packaged near the traditional single-sheet felt. Fleece fabric can be found in most fabric stores or you can purchase a 50" x 60"/127 x 152.4 cm fleece blanket from most discount stores for under $5. If your purse measures the same as the sample purse, 13"/33 cm across by 8"/20.5 cm high, you will need to cut a piece of felt or fleece about 12.5" x 15.5"/31.8 x 39.4 cm. The reason that the piece needs to be nearly double in height is because it will be folded in half, to line the front and back of the purse. The lining overall needs to be slightly smaller than the purse for a good fit. The nice feature about using felt or fleece is neither fabric will unravel when cut.

Fold the piece of felt or fleece in half and sew along both short edges using either a whipstitch, blanket stitch, or other comparable stitch with a needle and thread in a matching color. Insert the lining into your purse and whipstitch the top of the lining all along its edge to the front and back of the purse. Once completed, cut and weave in all ends.

Smartphone
Case

This pattern can be adapted to fit any size cell phone or tablet. An easy pattern that works up very quickly, it makes a nice gift for family and friends.

You can customize your case with a fancy button that will slip through one of the broomstick clusters or use another type of closure like a traditional snap. Work it up in a solid color as shown here or have some fun and add stripes.

Notes

- The case is crocheted as a single rectangle. It's then partially folded over onto itself and the edges seamed together to create the case. The top is folded over as a flap.

- The broomstick lace pattern is worked in single crochet (SC) in clusters of 3 loops.

YARN

100 yd/91.5 m soft worsted #4 weight yarn (shown in Berrocco® Comfort®, #9728 Raspberry Sorbet, 50% nylon, 50% acrylic; 210 yd/193 m, 3.5 oz/100 g per skein)

OTHER MATERIALS

- U.S. size G-6 (4 or 4.25 mm, depending on the brand) crochet hook, or size needed to obtain gauge
- U.S. size 17 (12 or 13 mm, depending on the brand) knitting needle or broomstick lace pin, 10"/25.5 cm or 14"/35.5 cm long
- Yarn needle
- Button or other closure
- Scissors

GAUGE

5 completed broomstick lace clusters x 6 rows completed broomstick lace clusters (12 rows total) = 3.5"/9 cm x 4"/10 cm

For a snug fit, gauge is important for this cell case. If you want to adjust the dimensions to fit a different sized phone or a tablet, you can increase or decrease the number of starting chains (be sure to do this in multiples of three for the broomstick lace pattern) for a narrower or wider cover and increase or decrease the number of rows to fit.

FINISHED MEASUREMENTS

3.5"/9 cm wide, 6"/15.2 cm long

Use your phone to measure where to fold over for the flap.

Case

With your crochet hook, CH 15. Measure this chain against
your cell phone. The chain should slightly hang over
both the right and left side of your phone for a correct
fit. If it does not, please read the sections on gauge
found on pages 39–40 and on page 76 to alter the
pattern to properly fit your cell phone.

Row 1: Slip the loop from the crochet hook onto the
knitting needle, then YO through the back loop of each
chain, pulling it through and onto the needle. At the end
of the row, you should have 15 loops.

Row 2: Insert the hook through the first 3 loops, YO, pull it
through, and CH 1. Slip the loops off the needle. Make 3
SC in the middle of them. *Slip the next 3 loops off the
needle. Make 3 SC in the middle of them.* Repeat
between * and * across the entire row. At the end of this
row, you will have completed 5 broomstick lace clusters.

Row 3: YO through the back loop of each SC, pulling it
through and up onto the knitting needle. You should
have 15 loops on your needle.

Row 4: Repeat Row 2.

Rows 5–40: Repeat Rows 3 and 4.

Cut the yarn, leaving a 24"/61 cm tail.

Finishing

Fold the cell case so that the cell phone fits correctly in the
case, with 1"/2.5 cm or more of the top part hanging
over to serve as the flap.

*Folding the case so that the starting chain is positioned on the
inside creates a more durable edge.*

Sew on any kind of button you like and use the center broomstick lace cluster on the flap as the buttonhole.

Depending upon your preferred method of sewing, you can either just sew along the edges while the case is facing the correct way, or you can turn it inside out and then sew along the edges. Thread a yarn needle with matching yarn and sew along both the right and left edges to form an enclosed case using a whipstitch or other comparable stitch. Weave in the ends. Turn the case right side out if necessary.

Sew a button to the inside part of the case and use the center hole of one of the broomstick lace clusters in the top flap as the buttonhole. Or sew on a purse clasp or other closure.

Wrap Skirt
or
Beach Cover-Up

This lacy open wrap skirt works up quickly and has a light, airy feel that is comfortable to wear in even the hottest weather. You can weave ribbon in and out at the top row to tie around your waist. Or, if you prefer, you can make the cover-up a pull-on skirt by weaving decorative elastic in and out at the top row and sewing or knotting the ends together. Make the skirt as long or as short as you wish.

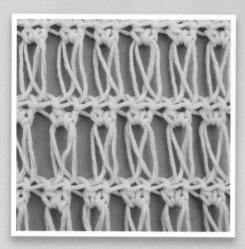

The skirt in the photos was made using 100% cotton yarn, which is soft and cool against the skin, perfect for a hot summer day. Linen, bamboo, and hemp would also work nicely. If you prefer the ease of 100% acrylic, feel free to use it.

SIZES

34"–36"/86.4–91.5 cm (37"–39"/94–99 cm, 40"–42"/ 101.6–106.7 cm, 43"–45"/109.2–114.3 cm, 46"–48"/ 117–122 cm, 49"–51"/125.5–129.5 cm)

YARN

300 yd/275 m (350 yd/320 m, 400 yd/366 m, 450 yd/412 m, 500 yd/457 m, 550 yd/503 m) fine #2 or DK #3 weight yarn (shown in Premier® Yarns Afternoon® Cotton Colors, #2201 White, 100% cotton; 136 yd/125 m, 1.8 oz/50 g per skein)

OTHER MATERIALS

- U.S. size H-8 (5 mm) crochet hook, or size needed to obtain gauge
- 1 or 2 U.S. size 50 (25 mm) knitting needles or broomstick lace pins, 14"/35.5 cm long (if you are making the 36"/91.5 cm hip size wrap, one knitting needle should suffice; for larger sizes you may find it easier to put half of the loops on one needle and half on a second needle)
- Yarn needle
- Scissors
- Up to 3 yd/2.75 m ribbon or decorative elastic, depending upon size
- Anti-fraying liquid

GAUGE

5 completed broomstick lace clusters x 2 rows completed broomstick lace clusters (4 rows total) = 3"/7.6 cm square
For proper fit, gauge is important for this wrap skirt.

Notes

- The broomstick lace pattern is worked in single crochet (SC) in clusters of 2 loops.
- A fine or DK weight yarn is recommended to get the right kind of drape. You certainly can make it using a heavier weight but it will be thicker and not have the same kind of soft flow. If you want to wear over leggings, a soft worsted weight yarn would work great.

FINISHED MEASUREMENTS

Hip Size	Width	Length
34"–36"/86.4–91.5 cm	36"/91.5 cm	12"/30.5 cm
37"–39"/94–99 cm	39"/99 cm	12"/30.5 cm
40"–42"/101.6–106.7 cm	42"/106.7 cm	12"/30.5 cm
43"–45"/109.2–114.3 cm	45"/114.3 cm	12"/30.5 cm
46"–48"/117–122 cm	48"/122 cm	12"/30.5 cm
49"–51"/125.5–129.5 cm	51"/129.5 cm	12"/30.5 cm

Skirt

With your crochet hook, CH 121 (131, 141, 151, 161, 171).

Bottom of Hemline: Skip the first chain and make 1 SC in each chain across. At the end of this row, you will have completed 120 (130, 140, 150, 160, 170) SC. Transfer the existing loop from your crochet hook onto your knitting needle.

Row 1: Slip the loop from the crochet hook onto the knitting needle, then YO through each SC across, pulling the loop through and onto the needle. At the end of the row you should have 120 (130, 140, 150, 160, 170) loops.

Row 2: Insert the hook through the first 2 loops, YO, pull through, and CH 1. Slip the loops off the needle. Make 2 SC in the middle of them. *Slip the next 2 loops off the needle. Make 2 SC in the middle of them.* Repeat between * and * across the entire row. At the end of this row, you will have completed 60 (65, 70, 75, 80, 85) broomstick lace clusters.

Rows 3–16: Repeat Rows 1 and 2.

Finishing

You can use the last broomstick lace cluster row that you made for weaving in the tie, or you can add one more row better suited for weaving in the ribbon:

Ribbon row: CH 3 and turn the work. Skip the 3 chains and HDC in the next stitch. *CH 1, skip the next stitch, and HDC in the next stitch.* Repeat between * and * across the row. Cut the yarn and weave in all ends.

Cut a length of ribbon that will fit properly around the wearer's waist, adding 10"/25.5 cm to 15"/38 cm or more for the tie. Using either the broomstick lace clusters or the spaces created by the ribbon row, weave the ribbon in and out along the upper edge. To keep the ends of the ribbon from unravelling, you can apply an anti-fraying liquid to them. You might also choose to use elastic instead of ribbon for a pull-on skirt. If this is the case, weave the elastic in and out of the spaces just like the ribbon, except you will not leave any excess elastic hanging at the end. Sew the two edges of the elastic together securely, and then spread the skirt over the sewn spot to conceal it. Block the skirt if needed.

Convertible Hair Band and Cowl

You can also wear this broomstick lace hair band (or head band) as a neck warmer. The band is worked in back-and-forth rows; it's a good first project if you've never worked in broomstick lace before. Once you become familiar with the process, you will find you can make several of these in one day!

Feel free to choose a solid-color yarn or a self-striping yarn with relatively slow color changes—too many color changes occurring too quickly sometimes distracts from the delicate flow of the stitch. Bold, bright colors are fun, while neutrals can be quietly sophisticated.

Since you only need 3 small buttons for this project, why not splurge and get something really special looking?

YARN

150 yd/138 m medium worsted #4 weight yarn (shown in Lion Brand® Vanna's Choice®, #171 Fern and #132 Radiant Orange, 100% acrylic; 170 yd/156 m, 3.5 oz/100 g per skein)

OTHER MATERIALS

- U.S. size H-8 (5 mm) crochet hook, or size needed to obtain gauge
- U.S. size 35 (19 mm) knitting needle or broomstick lace pin, 10"/25.5 cm or 14"/35.6 cm long
- Yarn needle
- Several buttons. Because the broomstick lace stitch automatically creates holes that can serve as buttonholes, you will have a maximum of 5 buttonholes to use; I like the look of only using 3. You might want to wait until after you have completed the band before purchasing buttons to make sure your selected buttons aren't too small or too big for the broomstick buttonholes. The versions shown in the photo both used 1"/2.5 mm buttons.
- Scissors

GAUGE

4 completed broomstick lace clusters x 4 rows of completed broomstick lace clusters (8 rows total) = 4"/10 cm square

If you're going to wear this as a headband, gauge is important to ensure a proper fit around your head.

FINISHED MEASUREMENTS

5"/12.7 mm wide, 20"/51 mm long

Notes

- In this pattern, the broomstick lace is worked in single crochet (SC) in clusters of 4 loops.
- It's easy to alter the size of this headband to fit anyone's head. To make the band smaller, just reduce the number of rows; to make it larger, add more rows.

Headband

With your crochet hook, CH 20.

Row 1: Slip the loop from the crochet hook onto the knitting needle, then YO through the back loop of each chain, pulling the resultant loop onto the needle. At the end of the row, you should have 20 loops.

Row 2: Insert the hook through the first 4 loops, YO, pull through, and CH 1. Slip the loops off the needle. Make 4 SC in the middle of them. *Slip the next 4 loops off the needle. Make 4 SC in the middle of them.* Repeat between * and * across the entire row. At the end of the row, you will have completed 5 broomstick lace clusters.

Row 3: YO through the back loop of each SC, pulling through and up onto the needle. At the end of the row, you should have 20 loops.

Row 4: Repeat Row 2.

Rows 5–40: Repeat Rows 3 and 4. Cut the yarn and weave in the ends.

Finishing

Sew the buttons on one of the edges of the band. Fold over the other side and ensure that everything lines up and you are able to button the band/cowl correctly. Cut and weave in all yarn ends used for sewing on the buttons.

It's so easy to add buttons to this; the broomstick lace cluster is open enough to function as a buttonhole.

So
Lacy
Wrap

This is a soft, lightweight wrap, perfect to wind around your neck or settle on your shoulders. It works up nicely in a soft cotton, or add a little nighttime pizzazz by using a yarn that contains metallic strands or sequins. Whatever yarn you use, I recommend that it be fine or DK weight. This will show off the openness of the broomstick lace stitch and produce a soft drape.

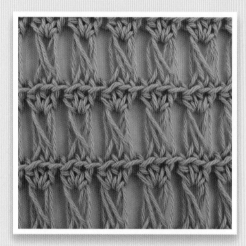

Notes

- The broomstick lace pattern is worked in half double crochet (HDC) in clusters of 3 loops.
- Feel free to alter the length of the wrap to your liking, crocheting fewer or more rows. Just be sure to end completing Row 4 so that the broomstick cluster is fully formed.
- The wrap shown in the photos is the smaller size.

Another option is to use a soft worsted weight yarn and a slightly larger crochet hook to create a thicker, heavier wrap. Also, you can leave off the fringe, if you prefer.

This works up nicely in a solid color or a self-striping yarn with relatively slow color changes, or you can crochet it with multiple colors in stripes.

SIZES
Small (Large)

YARN
275 yd/251.5 m (500 yd/503 m) fine #2 or DK #3 weight yarn (shown in Premier® Yarns Afternoon® Cotton Colors, #2204 Pastel Pink, 100% cotton; 136 yd/125 m, 1.76 oz/50 g per skein)

OTHER MATERIALS
- U.S. size F-5 (3.75 mm) crochet hook, or size needed to obtain gauge
- U.S. size 50 (25 mm) knitting needle or broomstick lace pin, 14"/35.5 cm long
- Yarn needle
- Scissors

GAUGE
3 completed broomstick lace clusters x 3 rows completed broomstick lace clusters (6 rows total) = 3"/7.6 mm long x 5"/12.7 mm high
Gauge isn't that important for this wrap unless you want the same dimensions as below.

FINISHED MEASUREMENTS
Small: 10"/25.5 mm wide, 75"/190.5 mm long, excluding fringe
Large: 20"/51 mm wide, 75"/190.5 mm long, excluding fringe

Wrap

With your crochet hook, CH 30 (60).

Row 1: Slip the loop from the crochet hook to the knitting needle, then YO through the back loop of each chain, pulling it through and up onto the needle. At the end of the row, you should have 30 (60) loops.

Row 2: Insert the hook through the first 3 loops, YO, pull through, and CH 1. Slip the loops off the needle. Make 3 HDC in the middle of them. *Slip the next 3 loops off the needle. Make 3 HDC in the middle of them.* Repeat between * and * across the entire row. By the end of the row, you will have completed 10 (20) broomstick lace clusters.

Row 3: YO through the back loop of each HDC, pulling it through and up onto the knitting needle. At the end of the row, you should have 30 (60) loops on your needle.

Row 4: Repeat Row 2.

Rows 5–90: Repeat Rows 3 and 4.

Finishing

Cut the yarn and pull the end through. Weave in the ends. You can leave the narrow ends as is or add fringe to them. Or, you can add it along one of the long sides instead. Cut eight 14"/35.5 mm lengths of yarn for each section of fringe. Holding all 8 pieces together at once, fold the combined yarn strands in half and insert the top loop part through one of the spaces between the broomstick lace clusters. Insert the remaining ends through the middle of this top loop and pull the ends to tighten and form a knot. The wrap shown has 9 sections of fringe along each of two edges for a total of 144 lengths of yarn. These numbers will be doubled for the large wrap. Trim the fringe so the pieces are all even.

You may want to block the wrap to ensure a neat, even appearance.

These gloves are more of an intermediate to advanced pattern. Fingerless mitts make for a fun, functional fashion statement, dressing up your hands while leaving your fingers free for texting or working the touchscreen on your tablet. You can place buttons or other fasteners on the inner wrist side for a snug fit and an elegant look. Cotton, acrylic, nylon, wool, and even bamboo yarn will produce beautiful results with this pattern.

YARN

175 yd/160 m fine #2 or DK #3 weight yarn (shown in Red Heart Crochet Nylon Size 18, Natural, 100% nylon; 150 yd/ 137 m per skein)

OTHER MATERIALS

- U.S. size F-5 (3.75 mm) crochet hook, or size needed to obtain gauge
- 2 or 3 U.S. size 19 (15 mm) knitting needles or broomstick lace pins, 10"/25.5 cm long
- Yarn needle
- Scissors
- Three 1/2"/1.3 cm buttons or other fasteners

GAUGE

3 completed broomstick lace clusters x 4 rows completed broomstick lace clusters (8 rows total) = 2.5"/6.4 cm wide x 4"/10 cm high
For a good fit, gauge is important for these gloves.

FINISHED MEASUREMENTS

4"/10 cm wide (at widest part), 6.5"/16.5 cm long

SPECIAL STITCHES

Reverse slip stitch: This stitch is the same as regular slip stitch, except the stitch is made in the opposite direction. Insert your hook under the designated stitch, yarn over, and pull through all the loops on your hook.

Notes

- The gloves are worked partly in rows, partly in the round; see page 30 for the tutorial Broomstick Lace in the Round.
- The broomstick lace stitch is worked in single crochet (SC) in clusters of 5 loops.

You can really dress these gloves up with stylish buttons at the wrist.

Right-Hand Glove

With your crochet hook, CH 35.

Row 1: Slip the loop from the crochet hook onto the knitting needle, then YO through the back loop of each chain, pulling it through and onto the needle. At the end of the row, you should have 35 loops.

Row 2: Insert the hook through the first 5 loops, YO, pull through, and CH 1. Slip the loops off the needle. Make 5 SC in the middle of them. *Slip the next 5 loops off the needle. Make 5 SC in the middle of them.* Repeat between * and * across the entire row. At the end of the row, you will have completed 7 broomstick lace clusters.

Row 3: YO through the back loop of each SC, pulling through and up onto the needle. At the end of the row, you should have 35 loops.

Row 4: Repeat Row 2.

Rows 5–8: Repeat Rows 3 and 4. At the end of Row 8, CH 4 and slip stitch to the first SC of the first cluster to join to work in the rnd.

Rnd 9: Slip the loop from the crochet hook onto one of the knitting needles. YO through the back loop of each of the 4 chains and all the SC around, pulling the loop through and up onto the needle. As you work around,

you will have to start drawing loops up onto the second knitting needle and then possibly a third to keep the loops from pulling. At the end of the rnd, you will have 40 loops on the needles.

Rnd 10: Insert the hook through the first 5 loops, YO, pull through, and CH 1. Slip the loops off the needle. Make 5 SC in the middle of them. *Slip the next 5 loops off the needle. Make 5 SC in the middle of them.* Repeat between * and * across the entire rnd. At the end of the rnd, you will have completed 8 broomstick lace clusters. Slip stitch to the first SC to join the rnd. Cut the yarn and weave in the ends.

Row 11: This row begins shaping the thumb section. Take note of the location of the slip stitch from the previous rnd. Count over 10 stitches to the right, or 2 full broomstick lace clusters. Join your yarn at the eleventh stitch, which is the first SC of the third broomstick lace cluster over from the slip stitch. Insert the crochet hook into the back loop of the stitch, YO, and pull the loop through and up onto the knitting needle. Repeat all the way around, switching to the other knitting needles if necessary. You should have 40 loops on your needle(s).

Row 12: Repeat Row 2. At the end of the row, you will have completed 8 broomstick lace clusters. Do not join.

Row 13: YO through the back loop of each SC, pulling it through and up onto the knitting needle. At the end of the row, you should have 40 loops.

Row 14: Repeat Row 2. You will have completed a total of 8 broomstick lace clusters. CH 4 and slip stitch to the first SC of the first cluster to join the rnd.

Rnd 15: Slip the loop from the crochet hook onto one of the knitting needles. YO through the back loop of each of the 4 chains and all the SC around, pulling the loop through and up onto the needle. As you work around, you will have to start drawing loops up onto the second knitting needle and then possibly a third to keep the loops from pulling. At the end of the rnd, you will have 45 loops on the needles.

Rnd 16: Insert the hook through the first 5 loops, YO, pull through, and CH 1. Slip the loops off the needle. Make 5 SC in the middle of them. *Slip the next 5 loops off the needle. Make 5 SC in the middle of them.* Repeat between * and * across the entire rnd. At the end of the rnd, you will have completed 9 broomstick lace clusters. Slip stitch to the first SC to join, then reverse slip stitch back to the last SC you made.

Rnds 17–18: Repeat Rnds 15–16 but after last slip stitch do not reverse slip stitch.

Cut yarn and weave in all ends.

Left-Hand Glove

Complete as for Right-Hand Glove through Rnd 10.

Row 11: This row begins shaping the thumb section. Take note of the location of the slip stitch from the previous round. Count over 4 stitches to the left. Join your yarn into the fifth stitch over to the left of the slip stitch, which is the first SC of the next broomstick lace cluster over from the slip stitch. Insert the crochet hook into the back loop of the stitch, YO, and pull the loop through and up onto the knitting needle. Repeat all the way around, switching to the other knitting needles if necessary. You should have 40 loops on your needle(s).

Complete as for Right-Hand Glove.

Finishing

Sew buttons or other fasteners to the underside of the gloves. The holes produced by the broomstick lace clusters can serve as buttonholes. Once completed, cut and weave in all ends.

Hoodie
Scarf

This hooded scarf is wonderfully warm for both children and adults. For the little kids, there are no long ends to get caught on something. For adults, you have a hat and scarf all in one, so there is no need to run around the house looking for one or the other!

Regarding yarn selection for this project, if you want the hood to be more drapey, use a softer yarn like Caron® Simply Soft. If you want it to hold its shape more, a yarn with a bit more texture to it, such as Lion Brand® Vanna's Choice®, is a better choice.

YARN
200 yd/183 m medium worsted #4 weight yarn (shown in Lion Brand® Vanna's Choice®, #304 Seaspray Mist, 100% acrylic; 170 yd/156 m, 3.5 oz/100 g per skein)

OTHER MATERIALS
- U.S. size H-8 (5 mm) crochet hook, or size needed to obtain gauge
- U.S. size 35 (19 mm) knitting needle or broomstick lace pin 14"/35.5 cm long
- Yarn needle
- Buttons or other fasteners or closures; the scarf shown used four ³/₄"/2 mm buttons
- Scissors

GAUGE
4 completed broomstick lace clusters x 4 rows completed broomstick lace clusters (8 rows total) = 4"/10 cm square
Gauge is important for the proper fit of this hooded scarf.

FINISHED MEASUREMENTS
Scarf section around the neck area, unbuttoned: 25"/63.5 cm long, 4"/10 cm high
Hooded section, folded in half: 8.5"/21.5 cm high, 10"/ 25.5 high
Total height from top of hood to bottom of scarf: 14"/ 35.5 cm

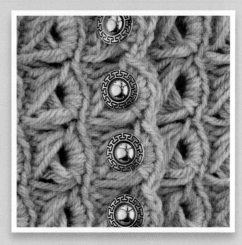

Notes

- The directions for this pattern are for an adult-sized hood. If you want to adjust the sizing down, you can work it using a U.S. size 19 (15 mm) knitting needle and a U.S. size G-6 (4 mm or 4.25 mm) crochet hook
- If you would like the hood to be shorter or taller to accommodate the size of your head or your hairstyle, you can crochet less or more than the 20 rows indicated. Just be sure you finish by completing Row 4.
- The broomstick lace pattern is worked in single crochet (SC) in clusters of five.

Back view of the scarf, and my new puppy, Bella.

Scarf Section

With your crochet hook, CH 20.

Row 1: Slip the loop from the crochet hook to the knitting needle, then YO through the back loop of each chain, pulling the resultant loop onto the needle. At the end of the row, you should have 20 loops.

Row 2: Insert the hook through the first 5 loops, YO, pull through, and CH 1. Slip the loops off the needle. Make 5 SC in the middle of them. *Slip the next 5 loops off the needle. Make 5 SC in the middle of them.* Repeat between * and * across the entire row. At the end of the row, you will have completed 4 broomstick lace clusters.

Row 3: YO through the back loop of each SC, pulling it through and up onto the needle. At the end of the row, you should have 20 loops.

Row 4: Repeat Row 2.

Rows 5–50: Repeat Rows 3 and 4.

Cut your yarn and weave in all ends.

Hood Section

Lay the scarf horizontally on the table, with its right side (public side) facing up toward you.

Count 5 full broomstick lace clusters from the right-hand side. Put a slip knot on your crochet hook and make 5 SC in the side of the fifth cluster. *Reach over to the next broomstick lace cluster and make 5 SC in the side of it.* Repeat between * and *, leaving four full broomstick lace clusters unworked at the left edge of the scarf. When you are done, there will be 4 full broomstick lace clusters left unworked at the right and left ends of the scarf and you will be ready to work 17 broomstick lace clusters centered on the scarf.

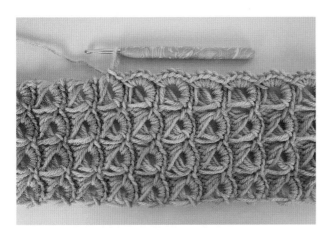

Working Row 1 of the hood section.

Row 1: Slip the loop from the crochet hook onto the knitting needle, then YO through the back loop of each of the SC, pulling it through and onto the needle. At the end of the row, you should have 85 loops.

Row 2: Insert the hook through the first 5 loops, YO, pull through, and CH 1. Slip the loops off the needle. Make 5 SC in the middle of them. *Slip the next 5 loops off the needle. Make 5 SC in the middle of them.* Repeat between * and * across the entire row. At the end of the row, you will have completed 17 broomstick lace clusters.

Row 3: Repeat Row 1.

Row 4: Repeat Row 2.

Rows 5–20: Repeat Rows 3 and 4.

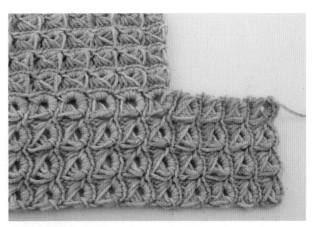

Completed scarf and hood section before being folded and seamed together at the top.

Cut your yarn, leaving an 18"/45.7 cm to 24"/61 cm tail for sewing closed the top of the hood.

Finishing

Fold the hood section in half and sew along the top edge using the yarn tail and yarn needle. You can use a whipstitch or other comparable sewing stitch. Cut and weave in all ends.

Sew the buttons onto the scarf section and use the holes produced by the broomstick lace clusters as buttonholes.

Dishcloth, Hot Pad, or Washcloth

You can use this project as a dishcloth, hot pad, or washcloth. The stitches are sturdy enough for everyday use, but the delicate look of the cloth makes it a nice choice for a housewarming or hostess gift.

In the fiber arts community, there is some debate on which fibers work best for dishcloths. Some people like 100% cotton yarn because the cotton encourages lathering of the soap and it is gentle on glassware and silverware. On the other hand, cotton can take a while to air-dry. Others prefer 100% acrylic yarn because it dries more quickly than cotton, making it less hospitable to the growth of bacteria or mold. And some acrylic yarns have a rougher texture, which works nicely to help clean food from the dishes.

If you intend to use this as a hot pad, other considerations come into play. Acrylic yarn can melt when brought into contact with very hot surfaces (like a pot just taken off the stovetop or out of the oven). Cotton yarn is more heat-resistant than acrylic, and 100% wool is even more heat-resistant.

YARN

100 yd/91.5 m medium worsted #4 weight yarn (shown in Red Heart® Super Saver®, #254 Pumpkin and #324 Bright Yellow—the striped cloth—and #672 Spring Green, 96% acrylic, 4% other fibers; 364 yd/333 m, 7 oz/198 g per skein)

OTHER MATERIALS

- U.S. size H-8 (5 mm) crochet hook, or size needed to obtain gauge
- U.S. size 19 (15 or 16 mm, depending on the brand) knitting needle or broomstick lace pin, 10"/25.5 cm or 14"/35.5 cm long
- Yarn needle
- Scissors

GAUGE

4 completed broomstick lace clusters x 4 rows completed broomstick lace clusters (8 rows total) = 4"/10 cm square
Gauge is only important in this pattern if you want to achieve the exact finished measurements below.

FINISHED MEASUREMENTS

8"/20.3 cm square

Notes

- The directions below are for crocheting the cloth in only one color, but you can add stripes if you like. Check the tutorial Changing Colors in Broomstick Lace on page 23 on how to switch yarns with a clean color break.
- The broomstick lace pattern is worked in single crochet (SC) in clusters of 4 loops.

Pattern

With your crochet hook, CH 32.

Row 1: Slip the loop from the crochet hook onto the knitting needle, then YO through the back loop of each chain, pulling it through and onto the needle. At the end of the row, you should have 32 loops.

Row 2: Insert the hook through the first 4 loops, YO, pull through, and CH 1. Slip the loops off the needle. Make 4 SC in the middle of them. *Slip the next 4 loops off the needle. Make 4 SC in the middle of them.* Repeat between * and * across the entire row. By the end of this row, you will have completed 8 broomstick lace clusters.

Row 3: YO through the back loop of each SC, pulling it through and up onto the knitting needle. You should have 32 loops on your needle.

Row 4: Repeat Row 2.

Rows 5–16: Repeat Rows 3 and 4.

Cut the yarn and weave in all ends.

Ballerina
Dress with
Tutu

This is such a fun project for your favorite little girl. The bodice is crocheted in broomstick lace stitch. I've provided directions for two ways to make the skirt: attaching strips of tulle to the bodice or making a separate skirt using an elastic waistband or ribbon.

Notes

- The broomstick lace pattern is worked in single crochet (SC) in clusters of 4 loops.
- Because this is meant to be a snug-fitting bodice, be mindful of how open your broomstick lace clusters are, particularly for an elementary school–aged girl. You can make your clusters less open by using a smaller size crochet hook. If the lace still ends up being more open than you prefer, you can sew a flesh-colored lining into the bodice.
- The bodice is worked flat, then finished with buttons in the back.
- It's easy to alter the size of this pattern by adding or subtracting stitches (be sure to do it in multiples of four so that the broomstick lace pattern will work) to increase or decrease the width of the bodice or by adding or subtracting rows to lengthen or shorten the torso.

You can find tulle in most any craft or discount store, usually in the special occasion or bridal section. Tulle that comes on 6"/15.2 cm plastic tube rolls is easier to work with than that sold in fabric stores on 54"/137 cm-wide bolts. It's available in a host of colors, as well as multicolor and with sparkles, glitter, and shiny and metallic finishes. You can make the skirt all one color, or have fun mixing it up. For added support if needed, you can use a piece of tulle to serve as a halter to hold the bodice in place, as shown in the photo.

SIZES
0–12 months (2–3 years, 4–5 years, 6–8 years)

YARN
Color A: 75 yd/69 m (115 yd/105 m, 150 yd/137 m, 190 yd/174 m) medium worsted #4 weight yarn (shown in Lion Brand® Vanna's Choice®, #102 Aqua, 100% acrylic; 170 yd/156 m, 3.5 oz/100 g per skein)

Color B: 25 yd/23 m (35 yd/32 m, 50 yd/46 m, 60 yd/55 m) medium worsted #4 weight yarn (shown in Lion Brand® Vanna's Choice®, #106 Little Boy Blue, 100% acrylic; 170 yd/156 m, 3.5 oz/100 g per skein)

OTHER MATERIALS
- U.S. size G-6 (4.0 or 4.25 mm, depending on the brand) crochet hook, or size needed to obtain gauge
- U.S. size 19 (15 or 16 mm, depending on the brand) knitting needle or broomstick lace pin, 14"/35.5 cm long
- Yarn needle
- Scissors
- 6 to 15 buttons or other fasteners or closure option. You will be able to use the broomstick lace clusters as buttonholes, so you may want to hold off purchasing the buttons until you verify the exact size that fits your stitches. The bodice in the photo used ³/₄"/2 cm buttons.
- Tulle. The exact amount will depend on the size and on how full and long a skirt your dancer prefers. The dress shown (6–8 years) used 2 full 40 yd/36.5 m rolls of 6"/15.2 cm tulle, for a grand total of 80 yd/73 m. One 40 yd/36.5 m roll should be sufficient for 0–12 months.
- ¹/₂"/1.2 cm-wide waistband elastic or ribbon (optional)
- Bows, flowers, charms, or appliqués to attach to the bodice (optional)

GAUGE

4 completed broomstick lace clusters x 5 rows completed
   broomstick lace clusters (10 rows total) = 4"/10 cm
   square
For proper fit, gauge is important for the bodice of the tutu.

FINISHED MEASUREMENTS
Bodice
*Width measured flat, unbuttoned; length measured from
   collarbone to below hipbone.*
0–12 months: Width, 19"/48.3 cm; length, 6"/15.2 cm

2–3 years: Width, 21"/53.3 cm; length, 8"/20.3 cm
4–5 years: Width, 23"/58.5 cm; length, 10"/25.5 cm
6–8 years: Width, 25"/63.5 cm; length, 12"/30.5 cm
Tulle Skirt
*Width measured flat, untied; length measured from waist to
   slightly past knees.*
0–12 months: Width, 19"/48.3 cm; length, 9"/23 cm
2–3 years: Width, 20"/50.8 cm; length, 12"/30.5 cm
4–5 years: Width, 22"/56 cm; length, 15"/38 cm
6–8 years: Width, 24"/61 cm; length, 18"/45.7 cm

Bodice

With your crochet hook and Color A, CH 76 (84, 92, 100).

Row 1: Slip the loop from the crochet hook onto the knitting needle, then YO through the back loop of each chain, pulling it through and onto the needle. At the end of the row, you should have 76 (84, 92, 100) loops.

Row 2: Insert the hook through the first 4 loops, YO, pull through, and CH 1. Slip the loops off the needle. Make 4 SC in the middle of them. *Slip the next 4 loops off the needle. Make 4 SC in the middle of them.* Repeat between * and * across the entire row. At the end of this row, you will have completed 19 (21, 23, 25) broomstick lace clusters.

Row 3: YO through the back loop of each SC, pulling through and up onto the knitting needle. You should have 76 (84, 92, 100) loops.

Row 4: Repeat Row 2.

Repeat Rows 3 and 4 using Color A until the bodice is 4 (6, 7, 8)"/10 (15, 18, 20) cm long. Attach Color B and continue repeating Rows 3 and 4 for an additional 2 (2, 3, 4)"/5 (5, 8, 10) cm.

Cut the yarn and weave in all ends.

Finishing

If possible, have the wearer try on the bodice. Note appropriate placement of the buttons for a snug fit. You might be able to place them along the edge of the bodice, or you may need to position them one or two broomstick lace clusters in. If you need to place them further in than that, consider adding two vertical rows of buttons. Sew the buttons onto the bodice.

Skirt

For the tutu, use the sizes listed under Final Measurements on page 101 as a guide for cutting the lengths of tulle, though you can make the skirt as long or short as you like and as full as you like. When cutting the lengths of tulle, they should be double the intended length of the skirt. After you cut the tulle, fold all the strips in half. You now have two options for creating the skirt.

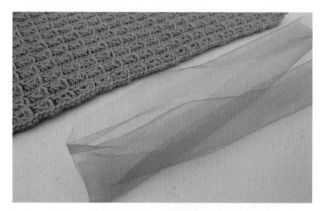

Fold the strips of tulle for the tutu in half.

Add the buttons along one back edge to secure the bodice.

Attaching the Tulle Directly to the Bodice

Insert the loop section of the folded length of tulle through the middle of one of the broomstick lace clusters.

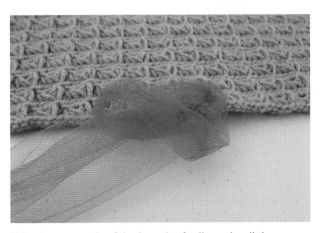

Take the two ends of the length of tulle and pull them through the loop.

Continue to pull on the ends until the loop end is snug up against the bodice.

Repeat all the way around the bodice, evenly spacing the tulle. If you like, you can combine 2, 3, or even 4 lengths of tulle and knot them all together through one of the broomstick lace clusters. This will produce a fuller skirt.

Making a Separate Skirt

While the bodice knotting method is a good choice for younger children, especially babies who might wiggle out of a detached skirt, older children usually prefer a separate skirt. To make one, cut a 36"/91.5 cm length of elastic or ribbon. Cut the tulle as previously described. Fold the tulle in half, and then instead of inserting it into a broomstick lace cluster, place it under the elastic or ribbon and pull the ends through the loop until it is snug up against the elastic or ribbon. Continue around in the same manner.

If you are using an elastic waistband, you can cut, pin, or sew the elastic ends together in the back. If you are using a ribbon, you can tie it into a bow in the back.

To make a separate skirt, attach the tulle to a length of ribbon or elastic as described for attaching it directly to the bodice.

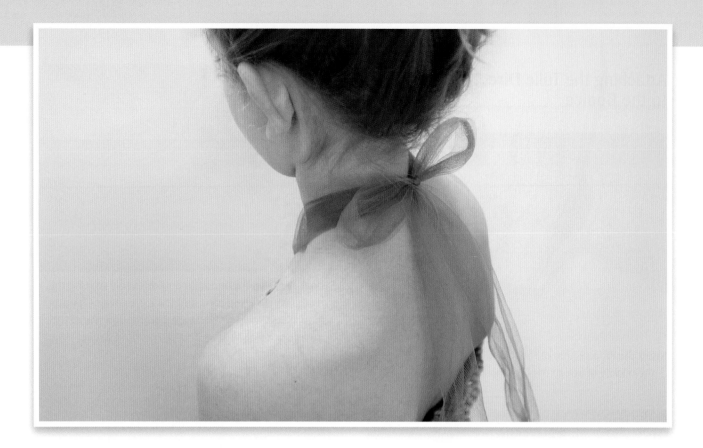

A completed skirt, using alternating light and dark turquoise tulle.

NOTE: If you are making this for a baby or young child, please take extra care that the child does not wrap the tulle strips around their neck.

Neck Strap (optional)

If the bodice is falling down on the recipient, it might help to knot a strip of tulle at the center of the front of the bodice. Cut one 18"/45.7 cm length of tulle. Following the same instructions as for attaching the tulle to the bodice, insert the loop section of the folded length of tulle through the middle of one of the broomstick lace clusters at the center front of the bodice and pull through. Use this as a strap that ties around the back of the neck.

Feel free to embellish the tutu bodice or skirt with bows, flowers, or other charms and accessories.

For a neck strap to support the bodice, attach a length of tulle at the center front broomstick lace cluster as directed for attaching it to the skirt.

Blanket

My grandmother made me a broomstick lace blanket when I was born, my first introduction to the stitch, so I had to include a blanket in this collection. This is a nice small throw, worked entirely in broomstick lace, that can be used as a lapghan or baby blanket.

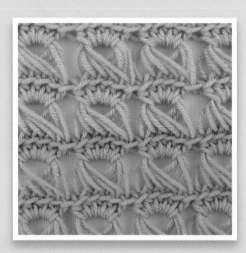

This blanket is guaranteed to receive many ooohs and ahhhs! It's easy to adjust the size—you can make it with fewer or more stitches to adjust the width (just make sure the total number of stitches is a multiple of five for the lace pattern) and fewer or more rows to make it shorter or longer.

Fiber choice is an important decision when making blankets. One hundred percent cotton blankets are extremely soft, gentle, and cool on the skin, providing just the right amount of warmth on a breezy summer evening. However, hand laundering a large cotton blanket such as this can be challenging. Cotton absorbs a tremendous amount of water, so your blanket will become very heavy once saturated with water, and squeezing the water out of it will take some muscle. Finally, you'll have to take care when laying it out to dry on towels that the lace stitches don't get stretched or distorted. One hundred percent wool (unless it is labeled machine washable) will also require hand laundering and the same care not to stretch or distort the stitches. Blankets made from 100% acrylic or a blend, on the other hand, are machine washable.

Notes

- Because of the large number of stitches involved, you will likely find it more comfortable to pull the loops up onto two knitting needles or onto a circular knitting needle.
- The broomstick lace pattern is worked in half double crochet (HDC) in clusters of 5 loops.
- Review the tutorial Changing Colors in Broomstick Lace (page 23); because the stripes are so wide, the yarn is cut at the end of each color band instead of being carried up the side as described in the tutorial.
- If you prefer, you can work the entire blanket in a single color. The total yarn needed to do that would be 1,456 yd/1,331 m.

YARN

Color A: 364 yd/333 m medium worsted #4 weight yarn (shown in Red Heart® Super Saver®, #512 Turqua, 96% acrylic, 4% other fibers; 364 yd/333 m, 7 oz/198 g per skein)

Color B: 364 yd/333 m medium worsted #4 weight yarn (shown in Red Heart® Super Saver®, #3251 Flame, 96% acrylic, 4% other fibers; 364 yd/333 m, 7 oz/198 g per skein)

Color C: 364 yd/333 m medium worsted #4 weight yarn (shown in Red Heart® Super Saver®, #324 Bright Yellow, 96% acrylic, 4% other fibers; 364 yd/333 m, 7 oz/198 g per skein)

Color D: 364 yd/333 m medium worsted #4 weight yarn (shown in Red Heart® Super Saver®, #672 Spring Green, 96% acrylic, 4% other fibers; 364 yd/333 m, 7 oz/198 g per skein)

OTHER MATERIALS

- U.S. size H-8 (5 mm) crochet hook, or size needed to obtain gauge
- 1 or 2 U.S. size 50 (25 mm) knitting needles or broomstick lace pins, 14"/35.5 cm long, or circular knitting needle
- Yarn needle
- Scissors

GAUGE

5 completed broomstick lace clusters x 3 rows completed
  broomstick lace clusters (6 rows total) = 7"/17.8 cm x
  5"/12.7 cm

*Gauge is less important for this blanket if you don't mind it
  being somewhat larger or smaller than the finished
  measurements below.*

FINISHED MEASUREMENTS

45"/114.3 cm square

Blanket

With your crochet hook and Color A, CH 160.

Row 1: Slip the loop from the crochet hook onto the
  knitting needle, then YO through the back loop of each
  chain, pulling it through and onto the needle. At the end
  of the row, you should have 160 loops. (When you reach
  about 80 loops, you might want to consider placing the
  remainder on a second knitting needle, if you're not
  using a circular needle.)

Row 2: Insert the hook through the first 5 loops, YO, pull it
  through, and CH 1. Slip the loops off the needle. Make 5
  HDC in the middle of them. *Slip the next 5 loops off the
  needle. Make 5 HDC in the middle of them.* Repeat
  between * and * across the entire row. At the end of the
  row, you will have completed 32 broomstick lace clusters.

Row 3: YO through the back loop of each HDC, pulling it
  through and up onto the knitting needle. You should
  have 160 loops.

Row 4: Repeat Row 2.

Row 5: Repeat Row 3.

Row 6: Insert the hook through the first 5 loops, YO, pull it
  through, and CH 1. Slip the loops off the needle. Make 5
  HDC in the middle of them. *Slip the next 5 loops off
  the needle. Make 5 HDC in the middle of them.* Repeat
  between * and * until the last set of 5 loops. Slip the
  loops off the needle, make 4 HDC in the middle of them.
  For the final HDC, YO, insert the crochet hook through
  the loops, YO, and pull through. Drop Color A. With the
  crochet hook, grab Color B and pull it through the 3
  loops remaining on the hook to complete the HDC. Cut
  Color A.

Row 7: Repeat Row 3.

Rows 8–12: Repeat Rows 2–6, dropping Color B and
  picking up Color C at the end of Row 6.

Row 13: Repeat Row 3.

Rows 14–18: Repeat Rows 2–6, dropping Color C and
  picking up Color D at the end of Row 6.

Row 19: Repeat Row 3.

Rows 20–24: Repeat Rows 2–6, dropping Color D and
  picking up Color A at the end of Row 6.

Repeat the 4 stripes.

Cut yarn and weave in all ends.

Triangle Kerchief Scarf

Triangular scarves are nice for several reasons. One, they are not as bulky to wear as a square scarf folded in half. Two, you can easily wear a triangle scarf as a neck scarf, a head scarf, or even as a shorter shawl. And three, you can practice another type of decreasing technique with broomstick lace using the reverse slip stitch method.

Instead of dividing clusters in half as I showed you how to do on page 28, a reverse slip stitch allows you to begin your next row one broomstick cluster over. This method creates a stair-stepped look to the sides of the scarf.

YARN

150 yd/138 m medium worsted #4 weight yarn (shown in Berrocco® Comfort®, #9724 Pumpkin, 50% nylon, 50% acrylic; 210 yd/193 m, 3.5 oz/100 g per skein)

OTHER MATERIALS

- U.S. size H-8 (5 mm) crochet hook, or size needed to obtain gauge
- U.S. size 35 (19 mm) knitting needle or broomstick lace pin, 10"/25.5 cm or 14"/35.5 cm long
- Yarn needle
- Scissors

GAUGE

3 completed broomstick lace clusters x 3 rows completed broomstick lace clusters (6 rows total) = 4"/10 cm square
Gauge isn't that crucial for this pattern unless you want it to be the exact size indicated below.

FINISHED MEASUREMENTS

40"/101.6 cm at its widest point, 14.5"/37 cm long

SPECIAL STITCHES

Reverse slip stitch: This stitch is the same as regular slip stitch, except the stitch is made in the opposite direction. Insert your hook under the designated stitch, yarn over, and pull through all loops on your hook.

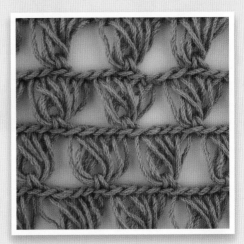

Notes

- An easy way to make the scarf larger is to use a U.S. size 50 (25 mm) needle.
- In this pattern, the broomstick lace is worked in single crochet (SC) in clusters of 5 loops.

Another way you can wear this scarf.

Scarf

With your crochet hook, CH 150.

Row 1: Slip the loop from the crochet hook to the knitting needle, then YO through the back loop of each chain, pulling it through and up onto the needle. At the end of the row, you should have 150 loops.

Row 2: Insert the hook through the first 5 loops, YO, pull through, and CH 1. Slip the loops off the needle. Make 1 SC in the middle of them. *CH 4. Slip the next 5 loops off the needle. Make 1 SC in the middle of them.* Repeat between * and * across the entire row. At the end of the row, you will have completed 30 broomstick lace clusters.

Row 3: Make 1 reverse slip stitch into each of the previous 4 chains. Make 1 reverse slip stitch into the top of the SC from the next to last broomstick lace cluster from the previous row. It is critical you take care to count the loops on this row, since there is a decrease in the number of loops. Slip the loop from the crochet hook onto the knitting needle, then YO through the back loop of each of the next 4 chains and pull through and up onto the needle. YO through the back loop of the next SC and pull through and up onto the needle. Continue drawing up loops in this way from the SC and chains, ending right before the SC in the second broomstick lace cluster from the end. You should have 135 loops on your needle.

Row 4: Insert the hook through the first 5 loops, YO, pull through, and CH 1. Slip the loops off the needle. Make 1 SC in the middle of them. *CH 4. Slip the next 5 loops off the needle. Make 1 SC in the middle of them.* Repeat between * and * across the entire row. At the end of the row, you will have completed 27 broomstick lace clusters.

Row 5: Repeat Row 3. You should have 120 loops on your needle.

Row 6: Repeat Row 4. At the end of the row, you will have completed 24 broomstick lace clusters.

Broomstick lace decreases created with the reverse slip stitch.

Row 7: Repeat Row 3. You should have 105 loops on your needle.

Row 8: Repeat Row 4. At the end of the row, you will have completed 21 broomstick lace clusters.

Row 9: Repeat Row 3. You should have 90 loops on your needle.

Row 10: Repeat Row 4. At the end of the row, you will have completed 18 broomstick lace clusters.

Row 11: Repeat Row 3. You should have 75 loops on your needle.

Row 12: Repeat Row 4. At the end of this row, you will have completed 15 broomstick lace clusters.

Row 13: Repeat Row 3. You should have 60 loops on your needle.

Row 14: Repeat Row 4. At the end of the row, you will have completed 12 broomstick lace clusters.

Row 15: Repeat Row 3. You should have 45 loops on your needle.

Row 16: Repeat Row 4. At the end of the row, you will have completed 9 broomstick lace clusters.

Row 17: Repeat Row 3. You should have 30 loops on your needle.

Row 18: Repeat Row 4. At the end of this row, you will have completed 6 broomstick lace clusters.

Row 19: Repeat Row 3. You should have 15 loops on your needle.

Row 20: Repeat Row 4. At the end of this row, you will have completed 3 broomstick lace clusters.

Row 21: Make 1 reverse slip stitch into each of the previous 3 chains. Slip the loop from the crochet hook onto the knitting needle. YO through the back loop of the next 4 stitches and pull through and onto the needle. You should have 5 loops on your needle.

Row 22: Insert the crochet hook through the 5 loops on the knitting needle, YO, pull through, and CH 1. Slip the loops from the needle and make 1 SC in the middle of them.

Finishing

Cut the yarn, pull the end through, and weave in all the ends. Block the scarf if needed.

Slouchy Hat

This pattern is quite versatile. You can convert it from a slouchy hat to a beanie by working fewer double crochet rows. Add buttons, bows, ribbons, and more along the band or a pom-pom at the top.

YARN

200 yd/183 m medium worsted #4 weight yarn (shown in Caron® One Pound™, #585 Lace, 100% acrylic; 812 yd/ 742 m, 16 oz/454 g per skein)

OTHER MATERIALS

- U.S. size H-8 (5 mm) crochet hook, or size needed to obtain gauge
- 2 or 3 U.S. size 35 (19 mm) knitting needles or broomstick lace pins, 14"/35.5 cm long
- Stitch markers
- Yarn needle
- Scissors

GAUGE

11 stitches x 6 rows of double crochet = 4"/10 cm square
Gauge is important for this hat if you want a good fit.

FINISHED MEASUREMENTS

Circumference: 22"/56 cm, height: 12"/30.5 cm

SPECIAL STITCHES

Reverse slip stitch: This stitch is the same as regular slip stitch, except the stitch is made in the opposite direction. Insert your hook under the designated stitch, yarn over, and pull through all the loops on your hook.

Notes

- The body of the hat is worked in double crochet (DC) in a spiral, or continuous round.
- The broomstick lace edging for the hat is worked in single crochet (SC) in clusters of 4 loops, in the round; please see the tutorial on Broomstick Lace in the Round on page 30.
- When working the broomstick lace edging in the round via slip stitching as opposed to a continuous spiral, a reverse slip stitch is required to reposition the hook back to the correct starting stitch prior to beginning the next round. Subsequent broomstick lace cluster rounds will then line up with previous ones.

Rnd 4: In the marked stitch, make 2 DC. In the next 2 stitches, make 1 DC. *In the next stitch, make 2 DC. In the next 2 stitches, make 1 DC.* Repeat between * and * around. You will have a total of 48 DC stitches once completed.

Rnd 5: In the marked stitch, make 2 DC. In the next 3 stitches, make 1 DC. *In the next stitch, make 2 DC. In the next 3 stitches, make 1 DC.* Repeat between * and * around. You will have a total of 60 DC stitches once completed.

Rnds 6–15: DC in marked stitch and in each stitch around, always marking the first stitch. You will have a total of 60 DC stitches once completed. Slip stitch to the next DC.

Broomstick Lace Edging

Rnd 1: Slip the loop from the crochet hook onto one of the knitting needles. YO through the back loop of each DC around, pulling the loop through and up onto the needle. As you work around the edge of the hat, you have to start drawing loops up onto the second knitting needle and then possibly a third to keep the loops from pulling. At the end of the rnd, you will have 60 loops on the needles.

Rnd 2: Insert the hook through the first 4 loops, YO, pull through, and CH 1. Slip the loops off the needle. Make 4 SC in the middle of them. *Slip the next 4 loops off the needle. Make 4 SC in the middle of them.* Repeat between * and * around. At the end of the rnd, you will have completed 15 broomstick lace clusters. Slip stitch to the first stitch of the first broomstick lace cluster. Make a reverse slip stitch back into the last SC stitch completed.

Rnd 3: YO through each SC around, pulling the loop through and up onto the needle. Use as many knitting needles as is needed to comfortably hold the loops.

Rnd 4: Repeat Rnd 2.

Rnds 5–6: Repeat Rnds 3–4, eliminating the reverse slip stitch on the last round.

Finishing

Cut the yarn and weave in all ends. Sew on any decorative elements, if you like.

Top Section of Hat

With your crochet hook, CH 4. This chain will not count as 1 DC stitch for any of the rnds in this pattern.

Rnd 1: Skip the first 3 CHs and make 12 DC in the fourth CH from the hook, marking the first DC with a stitch marker. Do not slip stitch.

Rnd 2: In the marked stitch, make 2 DC, marking the new first DC. *In the next stitch, make 2 DC.* Repeat between * and * around. You will have a total of 24 DC stitches once completed.

Rnd 3: In the marked stitch, make 2 DC, marking first DC. In the next stitch, make 1 DC. *In the next stitch, make 2 DC. In the next stitch, make 1 DC.* Repeat between * and * around. You will have a total of 36 DC stitches once completed.

Valance Café Curtain

This lovely lacy valance (or curtain valance) looks amazing when the light shines through it. You can weave a café curtain rod through the lace openings or use café curtain clips to hang it up in your window.

As for fiber choice, any will work, though you might think of choosing a yarn that is machine washable, particularly if it will be hanging in the kitchen.

Notes

- Because of the large number of stitches involved, you will likely find it more comfortable to pull the loops up onto two knitting needles or onto a circular knitting needle.
- The broomstick lace pattern is worked in double crochet (DC) in clusters of 5 loops.
- You can further adjust the width of the valance by increasing or decreasing the number of stitches (make sure that the final stitch count is a multiple of five so that the broomstick lace pattern works); the length can be made shorter or longer by decreasing or increasing the number of rows.

SIZES

30"/76 cm (36"/91.5 cm, 42"/106.7 cm, 48"/122 cm, 54"/137 cm)

YARN

300 yd/274.5 m (325 yd/297 m, 350 yd/320 m, 375 yd/343 m, 400 yd/366 m) medium worsted #4 weight yarn [shown in Bernat® Sheep(ish)™, Coral(ish), 70% acrylic, 30% wool; 167 yd/153 m, 3 oz/85 g per skein]

OTHER MATERIALS

- U.S. size H-8 (5 mm) crochet hook, or size needed to obtain gauge
- 1 or 2 U.S. size 19 (15 or 16 mm, depending on the brand) knitting needles or broomstick lace pins, 14"/35.5 cm long, or one 29"/73.7 cm circular knitting needle
- Yarn needle
- Scissors
- Café curtain rod in a size to fit your window or café curtain clips for hanging the valance (10 clips should be more than sufficient for a 42"/106.7 cm valance)

GAUGE

2 completed broomstick lace clusters x 2 rows completed broomstick lace clusters (4 rows total) = 3"/7.7 cm x 4"/10 cm

To get the proper size valance for your window, you'll want to pay attention to the gauge.

FINISHED MEASUREMENTS

The height for all the different widths is 16"/40.6 cm

Valance

With your crochet hook, CH 100 (120, 140, 160, 180).

Row 1: Slip the loop from the crochet hook onto the knitting needle, then YO through the back loop of each chain, pulling it through and onto the needle. At the end of the row, you should have 100 (120, 140, 160, 180) loops. Halfway through this process, you might want to put the balance of loops on a second knitting needle (if you're not using a circular needle) if the first needle becomes too crowded or too heavy.

Row 2: Insert the hook through the first 5 loops, YO, pull through, and CH 3. This CH 3 will count as a DC. Slip the loops off the needle. Make 4 DC in the middle of them. *Slip the next 5 loops off the needle. Make 5 DC in the middle of them.* Repeat between * and * across the entire row. At the end of this row, you will have completed 20 (24, 28, 32, 36) broomstick lace clusters.

Row 3: Slip the loop from the crochet hook onto the knitting needle, then YO through the back loop of each DC, pulling it through and up onto the knitting needle. Remember to include that CH 3 at the beginning of the previous row as an actual stitch that needs a loop drawn up from for this row. You will have a total of 100 (120, 140, 160, 180) loops.

Row 4: Repeat Row 2.

Rows 5–16: Repeat Rows 3 and 4.

Finishing

Cut the yarn and weave in the ends.

You can hang your curtain with the broomstick lace clusters facing up or down—both ways look pretty. In the photos shown here, the clusters are facing down.

Visual Index

Infinity Scarf   44

Pretty in Pink Pillow Cover   47

Boot Cuffs   52

Tote Bag   56

Baby Sweater   59

Baby Hat   63

Cutie Booties   67

Evening Bag   71

Smartphone Case   75

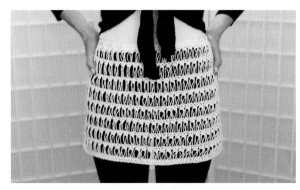

Wrap Skirt or Beach Cover-Up   79

Convertible Hair Band and Cowl   82

So Lacy Wrap   85

Fingerless Gloves   88

Hoodie Scarf   92

Dishcloth, Hot Pad, or Washcloth   96

Ballerina Dress with Tutu   99

Blanket   105

Triangle Kerchief Scarf   108

Slouchy Hat   112

Valance Café Curtain   115